# HOW UNEQUAL?

## Men and Women in the Irish Labour Market

A. Barrett, T. Callan (editor), A. Doris, D. O'Neill,
H. Russell, O. Sweetman, J. McBride

Oak Tree Press

Dublin

*In association with*

The Economic and Social Research Institute

Oak Tree Press
Merrion Building
Lower Merrion Street
Dublin 2, Ireland
www.oaktreepress.com

A catalogue record of this book is
available from the British Library.

ISBN 1 86076 191 7

This study forms part of The Economic and Social Research Institute's
General Research Series, in which it is Paper No. 176. It has been subject
to the normal internal and external refereeing procedures employed for
that series and accepted for publication by the Institute, which is not
responsible for either the content or the views expressed therein.

Printed in the Republic of Ireland by Colour Books Ltd.

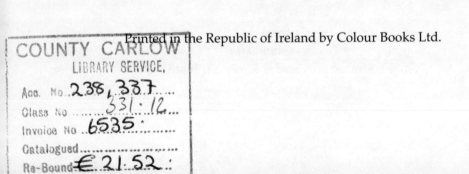

# Contents

# Tables and Figures

## FIGURES

# About the Authors

*Alan Barrett* is a Senior Research Officer at the Economic and Social Research Institute. He is a specialist in the analysis of labour market issues, and has published in a wide range of international journals. He obtained his PhD from Michigan State University in 1994 and has been a Research Affiliate of the Labour Economics Programme of the Centre for Economic Policy Research, London, since 1996.

*Tim Callan* is a Research Professor at the ESRI. He obtained his DPhil at the University of Oxford in 1989. His research interests include family policy, the labour market, income tax and social welfare policies, poverty and income distribution. He has a particular interest in bringing rigorous analytic methods to bear on current policy issues, including the development and application of *SWITCH*, the ESRI tax-benefit model.

*Aedín Doris* is a College Lecturer in the Department of Economics, NUI Maynooth. She studied at Trinity College Dublin and obtained her doctorate at the European University Institute, Florence. Her research interests lie in the area of labour economics, and in particular in empirical aspects of labour supply issues. Her publications include work on the labour supply of the wives of unemployed men, part-time working, and the effects of the minimum wage on labour force participation.

*Donal O'Neill* is a Senior Lecturer in Economics at NUI Maynooth. He obtained his PhD from the University of Iowa, USA. His fields of interest include the labour market, applied econometrics and economic growth. He has published on inequality, welfare and evaluations of labour market reform in several leading economics journals.

*Helen Russell* is a Research Officer at the ESRI. She obtained her DPhil from University of Oxford in 1997. Her main research interests include gender and the labour market, work attitudes, social change and social inequality. Recent publications have covered topics such as gender and the experience of unemployment, attitudes to employment across the EU, and lone parenthood.

*Olive Sweetman* is a College Lecturer in Economics at NUI Maynooth. She obtained her PhD from the University of Iowa in 1994. Her research interests include income distribution, poverty, equality of opportunity and intergenerational mobility, and have led to a number of publications on these topics in international journals.

*James McBride* was formerly a Statistical Analyst at the ESRI, and is now Director of the National Social Science Data Archive, a joint UCD-ESRI project. His interests include electoral politics, and quantitative methods in social science research.

# Acknowledgements

The authors have had the benefit of comments from many sources, using the ESRI's General Research Series reviewing procedures, and are grateful to all those who commented on earlier drafts. Starting closest to home, the authors would like to thank the Director, Brendan Whelan, the internal readers, Jerry Sexton and Chris Whelan, Brian Nolan, John FitzGerald and Philip O'Connell for their helpful comments and suggestions. Participants at a seminar in Autumn 1999 also gave valuable comments and criticisms. Insightful comments from an external referee are also gratefully acknowledged. We thank Bertrand Maitre for his assistance in analysing data for EU countries from the European Community Household Panel study. For his help with a number of technical issues, we also wish to thank John Walsh.

Financial support for the study came from the Department of Justice, Equality and Law Reform and is gratefully acknowledged. The study was undertaken in response to a commitment in Partnership 2000, and a committee representing the social partners and relevant government departments monitored the study's progress. Particular thanks are due to Joan Carmichael and to Sylda Langford for extensive comments which helped to improve successive drafts.

The study draws extensively on data from the 1994 and 1997 waves of the *Living in Ireland Survey*, the Irish element of the European Community Household Panel. For the 1994 wave, Brendan Whelan and James Williams of the ESRI's survey unit were responsible for the survey design, data collection and database creation. For the 1997 wave, James Williams and Dorothy Watson held the corresponding responsibilities.

Thanks are due to Merike Darmody, Pat Hopkins and Deirdre Whitaker for their patience, good humour and forbearance in processing the manuscript.

The editor would like to dedicate his work on this volume to Norah Callan, and to the memory of Maureen Callan.

# General Summary

## BACKGROUND TO THE STUDY

Women earn less, per hour, than men in most industrialised countries. How big is this gender gap in wages in Ireland? Why, 25 years after sex discrimination was outlawed, does a gender gap in hourly wages persist? How does this relate to the patterns of labour market participation by Irish women and men? What are the appropriate policy responses? These are among the key questions addressed by the present study, building on earlier ESRI work on this topic. The study was commissioned by the Department of Justice, Equality and Law Reform on behalf of a special Partnership 2000 Working Group which included representation from relevant government departments and the social partners.

## MEASURING THE OVERALL WAGE GAP

In Ireland, regular statistics on a full, economy-wide basis for male and female earnings are simply not available. For this reason, undue reliance is often placed on the regularly published series for hourly earnings of men and women in manufacturing. But more than four out of five women work *outside* the manufacturing sector. For this reason, statistics on hourly earnings in manufacturing, however accurate and interesting in themselves, cannot provide a guide to either the level or the trend in the economy-wide gender wage gap.

For a fuller picture, we must rely on the special surveys undertaken by the ESRI. A baseline picture of economy-wide wage differentials in 1987 was already produced using the Survey of

Income Distribution, Poverty and Usage of State Services (Callan and Wren, 1994). The present study aimed to bring that picture up to date using information from the first (1994) wave of the *Living in Ireland Survey*, the Irish element of the European Community Household Panel. It has also proved possible to draw on some more recent information from the 1997 wave of the *Living in Ireland Survey*.

The ESRI survey data show that average hourly earnings of women in 1987 were about 80 per cent of those of the average man. By 1994, this ratio had risen to just over 82 per cent, with a further rise to 84.5 per cent by 1997. These ratios are about 13 percentage points higher than the corresponding ratios in manufacturing. Men in manufacturing have a wage which is reasonably representative of the wages in the wider economy, but women in manufacturing tend to occupy lower-waged jobs than women outside manufacturing.

A special analysis revealed that men were more likely than women to have jobs which included a range of benefits. The most valuable of these is likely to be a pension. When this is taken into account, the gap between men's and women's overall compensation per working hour is 1 or 2 percentage points wider than when only cash earnings are considered.

### STRUCTURE OF THE WAGE GAP

A part of this observed wage gap is simply due to differences in the labour-market-relevant characteristics of men and women in paid employment. For example, we know that wages tend to rise with age and labour market experience. But the average woman worker has worked 12 years in the paid labour market, as against 18 years for the average man. Using widely applied statistical techniques, we can decompose the total wage gap into a part which is explained by such differences (e.g. in age, labour market experience or education) and leaving a portion which is unexplained. This analysis shows that about half of the total wage gap in 1987 was explained mainly by differences in labour market experience. By the 1990s, however, almost three-quarters of the gap was explained by such factors.

The "unexplained" wage gap is sometimes treated as the basis for calculating how much higher the average female wage would be "if a woman were paid like a man". It must be recognised, however, that this may give a false impression of how precisely one can measure labour market discrimination. The figure arrived at may be higher or lower than the actual level of discrimination for a number of reasons. No survey can possibly contain data on all the labour-market-relevant characteristics of each employee; the "unexplained" gap might be due to unobserved or unmeasured productivity-relevant characteristics. On the other hand, women facing discrimination (even if it arises outside the labour market) may rationally decide to spend less time in the labour market, thereby reducing their potential future wage. However, the calculation of the so-called "discrimination index" is a useful summary in making comparisons over time and across countries.

The so-called "discrimination index" stood at about 15 per cent in 1987, i.e. the average woman would have earned about 15 per cent more if her characteristics were rewarded in the same way as men's. By the 1990s, however, the index of "discrimination" had fallen to about 5 per cent. Thus, the modest observed rise in women's wages relative to men's concealed a more significant shift in the earnings structure. The "discrimination index" of 5 per cent compares quite favourably with that in the UK and other EU countries.

Why, if the "discrimination index" was falling by about 10 percentage points, did the observed gender wage gap not fall by the same amount? In part this reflects changes in labour market structure over the period, with a substantial increase in overall wage inequality. As women have tended to be over-represented among the low paid, the shift in the wage structure towards greater vertical inequality has worked to women's disadvantage. Despite this, women's wages have progressed relative to men's, but this gain has been achieved while women were "swimming against the tide" in terms of the increase in overall wage inequality, over the 1987 to 1994 period.

## POTENTIAL CAUSES OF THE GAP

What are the causes of the 5 per cent wage gap, which cannot be explained on the basis of labour market characteristics measured in the survey? Some would argue that the wage gaps arise because sex discrimination lives on "underground", in an illegal fashion, and that more vigorous enforcement is needed. Others would argue that existing laws are well enforced but that the law is too narrow to cope with more sophisticated forms of sex discrimination. Viewed from another angle, some part of the gap in wages may arise because of a long shadow cast by earlier discrimination, including the marriage bar. Even when such discrimination is removed, it can have long-lived effects: higher levels of management and some entire professions may remain male-dominated. One result may be that girls and younger women do not see female role models in senior positions in certain professions or in higher-level management within some organisations. Even in times when the typical male and female roles are changing rapidly, personal and social expectations can be heavily influenced by the long-established norm of husband as breadwinner and wife as housewife — to such an extent that when women break out of the earlier stereotype, they may find themselves expected to simply add their new role as active participants in the paid labour market on top of the traditional "home-making" role.

## EARNINGS AND LABOUR MARKET PARTICIPATION

If the objective of policy were simply to close the gap in hourly wages between men and woman (rather than the actual goal of equality of opportunity), the trend towards women staying attached to the paid labour market during the child-bearing and child-rearing years would have to continue. This raises complex economic and social issues, some of which fall outside the scope of the current study. Here we are concerned with the factual situation regarding links between labour market participation and pay.

Analysis of the factors influencing labour market participation shows that it is the arrival of children that leads to the crucial differences in participation. It is found that participation decisions following the arrival of one child when aged 26 and another when aged 29 will lead, by the time the second child is 18, to a typical woman (with the same educational qualifications as a typical man) having nine years less labour market participation than her male counterpart. This has a major effect on the wage that can be commanded in the labour market. The wage paths for the man and woman cannot be brought closely into line without a further increase in labour market attachment of women during the child-bearing and child-rearing years.

One way of achieving such an increase in labour market attachment in a "family-friendly" fashion is through part-time working. A key issue here is whether part-time workers experience a wage penalty because of an imbalance between the supply of, and demand for part-time workers. Statistical analysis reveals no significant evidence of such a penalty in Ireland in 1994.

## SELECTED POLICY ISSUES

While high-quality, affordable childcare is often seen as a *sine qua non* for true equality of opportunity, childcare policy must be designed with more than this in mind: the interests of children are central, and policy must be geared to facilitating individual choices either to stay in the paid labour market or to take time out to care for children (and indeed for other family members). Equality of opportunity, rather than complete equality of outcome, is the declared aim of government policy. Even with a fully funded high quality childcare system, some sex differences in labour market participation could be expected. But the present situation is far from that point. The Commission on the Family has pointed to this lacuna in the state's investment strategy, calling for an increased investment in the care of its youngest citizens. Whether this care should be provided by parents, or purchased by them from high quality providers is, we would contend, essentially a choice best left to the parents. State support should, we believe, be broadly neutral as between different modes of care: parents rather than the state are best placed to decide what suits their child and their family.

A wide range of other measures are also relevant to the equalisation of opportunities. Recent legislation on equality and the nature of its implementation will play a significant role; the internal structure of trade unions and the nature of bargaining with employers and in a social partnership framework will also be important. The introduction of a National Minimum Wage will also have helped to close the pay gap; particular attention must be given in future to how this wage is to be uprated. Measures designed to make the workplace more family-friendly will also play a role: these would include parental leave, maternity leave, and, a key factor in the current environment, assistance for women re-entering the job market after a period of full-time work in the home. In addition, measures designed to reduce "vertical gender segregation" would help to reduce the wage gap.

## SOME POLICY IMPLICATIONS

If, on average, women are likely to have a shorter job tenure than men, and if there are additional costs associated with the employment of women (e.g. costs of maternity leave), then a profit-maximising employer may have an incentive to hire or promote a man instead of an equally well-qualified woman. This would be illegal under Irish law. But the nature of this economic incentive means that the price of equality, like that of liberty, is eternal vigilance. Even if discrimination has been reduced to low levels, this should not lead to complacency.

We see a need for regular monitoring at four levels:

- At *national* level, the basic statistical requirement is a large, regular household survey with detailed labour market information from each adult, including earnings and hours worked. This need can be filled either by a regular cross-section survey with such information (e.g. by adding questions on earnings to the Labour Force Survey) or by an annual panel survey such as the ESRI's *Living in Ireland Survey*.

- At *sectoral* level it may be possible to gather information in other ways; for example, by having some common reporting requirements, a databank could be built up in the public service which would enable a more intensive monitoring of equality issues in future.

- At *firm* level, the key issues include processes of recruitment and promotion, and how staff are allocated to tasks involving a training component or to training courses. Here again, there is a role for common reporting requirements, but also for equality audits by quality-approved analysts, on the direction of the Equality Authority.

- *Individual cases* investigated by the Office of Equality Investigations should also be monitored to keep track of trends and problem areas; patterns may arise across cases which can be dealt with more effectively at a higher, policy level, than by "firefighting" the cases as they arise.

The economic incentive to discriminate can be seen as similar to the economic incentive to evade taxes: it may, in some circumstances, be cheaper to discriminate (e.g. hire a man rather than a somewhat more qualified woman), just as it is cheaper in cash terms to evade a tax liability. But most taxpayers are compliant. Developing a culture of compliance may be more effective than a "big brother" approach to monitoring. Equality audits can act both as a "stick" (somewhat like a tax audit) but also have a more positive function in helping employers to understand and deal with hidden sources of discrimination. It is important that compliance costs should be kept to a reasonable level, in order to avoid unnecessarily raising the costs of employment.

In terms of progress to date, the results suggest that the degree of discrimination in the Irish labour market has fallen between 1987 and 1994. On average, women's hourly wages are now about 85 per cent of the average male wage. About three-quarters of the gap between men's and women's hourly wages can be attributed to the fact that women, under current social and economic structures, typically spend less time in the labour market than men and more time as carers in the home. Unless men and women were to become much more similar in this respect — and views will differ on whether or not this should happen — then complete equality of labour market outcome is not the appropriate yardstick for a policy aiming at equality of opportunity.

*Chapter 1*

# Introduction

It is now 25 years since sex discrimination in pay was outlawed. In the early years following the enactment and enforcement of equality legislation, women's wages rose relative to men's. But there is still a substantial gap between the pay of the average woman and that of the average male employee. Why? Is it because sex discrimination lives on in illegal and underground forms? Is it because the law is not strict enough, or that enforcement is lacking? Or does the gap reflect differences in labour market participation, in which case it is the sources of such differences that must be investigated? These are among the central questions investigated by this study, which answers the need for a follow-up study to Callan and Wren (1994), as identified in Partnership 2000.

The issues dealt with in the volume are complex and definitive answers cannot be provided on some questions — even when, as in some other countries, the volume of research on the topics is quite enormous. But research can shed light on the extent and nature of the gap, and provide insights which can inform policy judgements. This is what the present study aimed to do, building on what was learned from the earlier study based on 1987 data. The present report brings much of that analysis up to date (with data from 1994 and 1997); analyses the causes of the changes in the wage gap since 1987; and extends the earlier study in several directions (suggested by insights gained from the 1987 study and/or current policy concerns).

The report is structured as follows. Chapter 2 describes how the economy-wide differences between male and female average wages have evolved between 1987 and 1994, and how these dif-

ferences are structured in terms of the characteristics of job hold-
ers (such as age, labour market experience, educational qualifications). Additional information on the male-female wage ratio for
1997 is also included. Chapter 3 goes on to decompose the 1994
male–female wage differential into a part which can be explained
by differences in individual characteristics (such as length of labour market experience), and a "residual" which is often treated
as a measure of potential discrimination in the labour market.
Again, similar information is provided for 1997. Chapter 4 broadens the analysis to take into account non-pay elements of the
compensation package, and considers a number of conceptual and
sectoral issues in interpreting the results. Chapter 5 reviews available evidence on the international comparison of gender wage
gaps. Chapter 6 goes beyond consideration of gaps in average
wages to consider issues related to the distribution of wages for
men and women, and the potential direct impact of a national
minimum wage on the gender wage gap. Chapter 7 discusses
some of the issues relating to labour force participation. Chapter 8
considers policy issues in the light of the findings from earlier
chapters, and the international literature on these issues. Chapter
9 draws together the main findings and policy implications.

## APPENDIX 1.1: TERMS OF REFERENCE FOR THE WAGE DIFFERENTIAL STUDY

Investigate the following:

a. Repeat the analysis of Chapters 3 and 4 of the 1994 study using data from the 1994 *Living in Ireland Survey*.

b. Examine the wage gap, both on the basis of the 1994 study and the 1994 data, to refine information on the reasons which underlie it and the relative contribution of each underlying reason to the gap.

c. Explore the potential for "within sector" analysis, using existing datasets to identify the extent of and reasons for the wage gap on a sectoral basis, and advise on what additional data would help to make further progress in this area.

d. Examine and quantify sex differences with regard to pensions provision and fringe benefits.

e. Examine and quantify the factors affecting male and female labour force participation, focusing particularly on the impact of family responsibilities, and the links between labour force participation and pay.

f. Examine the distribution of hourly wage rates for men and women, and identify the potential immediate impact of minimum wage rates at various levels.

g. Undertake comparisons with other EU countries and seek to identify factors contributing to cross-country differences in wage differentials.

h. Consider the implications of the findings for policy purposes.

*Chapter 2*

# Male/Female Wage Differentials: A Statistical Profile

## 2.1 INTRODUCTION

Ireland, like many other countries, has legislation which seeks to guarantee "equal pay for equal work", as between men and women. Despite this legislation, there remain, in most countries, gaps between the average wages of men and women. How large are the gaps? How can they be explained? Why do they vary across countries and over time and between groups of workers? An exploration of these questions is essential for the design and implementation of appropriate and effective policy interventions.

We begin our study of these issues by summarising some basic information about the size and structure of the gap between men's and women's wages in Ireland. We focus in particular on the years 1987 and 1994, for which comprehensive economy-wide information on male and female hourly wage rates is available from suitable household surveys. Thus, the present chapter updates the information on the size and structure of the wage gap presented in Callan and Wren (1994). In the following chapter, we address this issue of possible discrimination more formally and more systematically, when we decompose the gender wage gap into different components, again following the approach taken by Callan and Wren, to facilitate comparisons of the change in the size and structure of the wage gap over the 1987 to 1994 period.

## 2.2 PREVIOUS RESEARCH

Prior to the publication of Callan and Wren's study in 1994, research on the gender wage gap in Ireland had been restricted by a lack of suitable data. Although studies had looked at differences in the wages of men and women, only sub-groups of the population of employees were examined and so no overall picture of the female/male wage differential existed.

Blackwell's (1986) analysis of the male/female differential provides a good example of the limitations of the earlier work. His work was based on two main data sources; statistics on the earnings of industrial workers published by the Central Statistics Office and statistics on the structure and distribution of earnings for 1974 and 1979 published by Eurostat. As the CSO statistics concentrated on workers in industry, they excluded individuals working in agriculture, building and construction, public administration, retail and wholesale distribution, finance and professional and personal services. Given that only one-third of workers are employed in industry, it is clear that any wage comparisons based on this group will not be representative of all workers.

Blackwell's other data sources were the Surveys of the Structure and Distribution of Earnings which were conducted in 1974 and 1979. The 1974 survey covered wholesale and retail distribution, and banking and insurance; for the 1979 survey, industry was added. As a result, this 1979 survey was broader in its coverage of employees than the CSO data but it was still limited from the point of view of establishing and analysing economy-wide figures on male/female wage differentials. This was because it excluded almost two-thirds of employment in the total services sector, in which female employment is more heavily concentrated.

The Callan and Wren (1994) study overcame these limitations by using a nationally representative dataset, which included employees in all sectors and in all sizes of firm. The data were drawn from ESRI's Survey of Income Distribution, Poverty and Usage of State Services, conducted in 1987. A similar survey — the *Living in Ireland Survey* — was conducted by the ESRI in 1994, as part of the European Community Household Panel (ECHP). As much of the analysis in this report is based on these two surveys, we describe each of them in turn in the next section.

## 2.3 DATA SOURCES

### Survey of Income Distribution, Poverty and Usage of State Services, 1987

A full description of the 1987 survey is contained in Callan, Nolan et al. (1989); here we concentrate on the main features relevant to the analyses undertaken in the present study.

The sampling frame for the 1987 survey was the Electoral Register. A sample of names and addresses was drawn using the RANSAM programme, whereby each individual on the register had an equal probability of selection (Whelan, 1979). This procedure implied that larger households were more likely to be selected than smaller households, but a reweighting procedure (outlined below) was used to ensure that the resultant data were nationally representative of all households.

Interviews were obtained from a total of almost 3,300 households — a response rate of 64 per cent of the effective sample. In order to correct for possible biases introduced by the pattern of non-responses the sample was reweighted using information from the 1986 Labour Force Survey. The reweighting was based on a four-way cross-tabulation: number of adults in the household, urban versus rural location, and the age and occupation of the household head. Reweighting the sample ensured that it represented the distribution of the population of households over the cells in this four-way classification in the same way as the 1986 *Labour Force Survey*.

In addition to the questionnaires which sought information on the household, a detailed individual questionnaire was also given to people aged 15 and over who were not in full-time education. This individual questionnaire asked for information on labour market issues such as current earnings and other income, labour market experience, level of education, occupation and industry. By combining questions on usual gross pay and usual hours worked, it was possible to calculate hourly wage rates for the 2,763 employees in the sample. It was these hourly wage rates that were used to measure and analyse the male/female wage differential.

Following the reweighting procedure, it was possible to check the reliability of the ESRI survey data in terms of how well it represented the population; this was done by comparing predicted totals and proportions with independent information from sources such as the Census of Population and the distribution of income revealed in the Statistical Report of the Revenue Commissioners. Such checks supported a high level of confidence in the reliability of the survey information and so we can have confidence in the reliability of the figures on the gender wage gap.

## Living in Ireland Survey, 1994

Much of the analysis in the present study is based on the ESRI's *Living in Ireland Survey*, 1994. This is the first wave of the Irish element of the European Community Household Panel, which in turn is a series of household surveys being conducted throughout the EU. As with the 1987 survey, the sampling frame was again the Electoral Register. The survey had a response rate of 64 per cent, allowing information to be obtained from 4,048 households. Again following the approach used in 1987, the sample has been reweighted to correct for non-response on the basis of the number of adults in the household, urban/rural location, age and socio-economic group of the household head, using information from the Labour Force Survey. The overall representativeness of the sample data has been validated by comparison with a variety of external information and on this basis it appears to represent the target population well in terms of, for example, age and sex, household composition and taxable income.

The survey sought detailed information on the earnings, education, labour market experience and other characteristics of employees in the households surveyed; the sample contains over 3,000 employees who responded fully to the relevant labour market questions. Of particular relevance here is that employees were asked about the gross pay they received in their last pay period, and about how long this covered (week, fortnight, month, etc.) and the hours worked during that period. They were also asked whether this was the amount they usually receive, and if not what was their usual gross pay and hours worked. Combining this information, gross hourly wages have been calculated and it is on these figures that we base most of our analysis.

The existence of a nationally representative sample for 1987 allowed Callan and Wren to establish and analyse the economy-wide gender wage differential for the first time. The 1994 sample now allows us to consider the trend in the national differential, again for the first time. Given the ongoing efforts to achieve greater gender equality in Ireland, an analysis of the trend is clearly important in monitoring progress in this area.

## 2.4 THE MALE/FEMALE WAGE GAP, 1987–1994

We now turn to the data and begin our analysis of the male/female wage differential in 1994 and the comparison with what it was in 1987. We firstly look at the differential for all employees before looking at the differential across various subgroups. It will be seen that the particular subgroups we look at are those which were considered in the earlier work (from here on referred to as the 1987 study) because we are interested in being able to make direct comparisons over time; however, these subgroups are also of intrinsic interest, just as they were in 1987, because they relate to characteristics that determine wage rates, such as age, education and labour market experience.

In Table 2.1, the average hourly wages of male and female employees in 1994 are shown, along with the ratio of female-to-male hourly wages and the corresponding ratio from 1987. We compare results from the ESRI survey, representing all employees, and the CSO data on hourly industrial earnings, as reported in the *Irish Statistical Bulletin* (1995). The ESRI figures show a slight rise in the female-to-male wage ratio on an economy-wide basis, from 80.1 per cent in 1987 to 82.4 per cent in 1994.

In introducing this chapter, we made reference to the need to have a sample of all employees in order for an accurate picture of the economy-wide female/male wage ratio to be produced; this point is well illustrated in Table 2.1. In both 1987 and 1994, the gender wage gap for all employees is much smaller than that for industrial workers in industry. As noted in the Callan and Wren study, industrial workers in industry comprised less than one in three of all employees, and less than one in five of female employees in 1987.

## Table 2.1: *Average Hourly Earnings of Men and Women*

|  | Female-to-Male Wage Ratio | | Hourly Wage, 1994 | |
|---|---|---|---|---|
|  | *1987 (%)* | *1994 (%)* | *Men* | *Women* |
| ESRI: All employees | 80.1 | 82.4 | £7.75 | £6.39 |
| CSO: Industrial workers in industry | 67.6 | 72.7 | £6.99 | £5.08 |

*Note:* The ESRI figures for 1994 are based on a total of 3,305 employees (1,915 men and 1,390 women). The figures reported above are weighted, as described in the preceding section, to ensure that they are representative of key characteristics of the population. The same comments apply to the other tables in this chapter. The CSO figures are taken from the series on Industrial Earnings, Employment and Hours Worked published in the *Irish Statistical Bulletin* (1995).

There is no particular reason why the wage levels or female–male wage ratio for this sub-group should be representative of the level or trend in wages and wage ratios for all employees. Table 2.1 shows that the level of the female–male wage ratio is between 10 and 13 percentage points higher (in 1994 and 1987 respectively) for all employees than for the sub-group of industrial workers in industry. Furthermore, we find that while the female-to-male wage ratio has risen by just over 5 percentage points for industrial workers in industry, the economy-wide rise in the ratio has been much smaller, at 2.2 percentage points. The changes within the group of industrial workers in industry are, of course, of interest; but our primary concern is with understanding how the male–female wage gap has developed for all employees, economy-wide.

A small rise in the economy-wide female-to-male wage ratio, as observed here, can be consistent with quite different underlying developments. In the remainder of this chapter, and elsewhere in this report (particularly in Chapters 3 and 5), we seek to disentangle the different influences that have led to this limited rise in the female-to-male wage ratio. But as we present some further evidence on the evolution of the size and structure of the wage gap, it is useful to bear in mind some of the potentially conflicting influences on the overall female-to-male wage ratio. The average male and female wages depend on the average characteristics of male and female employees, and on the average rewards men and women receive for similar labour-market-relevant characteristics (such as educational qualifications or length of labour market experience). A rise in female relative to male wages could arise either from enhanced labour market characteristics of women, or from a situation in which the rewards for women were improving relative to men, while the labour market characteristics of the average woman were unchanged or even becoming less favourable relative to those of the average man. This approach is described and applied more systematically in the next chapter, but we mention it here to guard against potentially misleading interpretations of some of the material presented in the present chapter.

## 2.5 THE STRUCTURE OF THE MALE/FEMALE WAGE GAP

We can look more closely at the differential by looking at the female/male ratio across different subsets of the population of employees. Subdividing the dataset in this manner can lead to small numbers of observations in certain cells, for which the margin of error attached to our estimates of average wages or wage ratios would be unacceptably high. For this reason we follow the approach used in the 1987 study of omitting cells with less than 25 observations and placing an asterisk beside cells with 25 to 50 observations.

Over the life-cycle, men's and women's labour market participation tends to differ. In particular, it has normally been the case that women have been more likely to have breaks in their labour market experience due largely to childbirth and child-rearing. For this reason, it is instructive to consider the female/male wage ratio across age groups and this is done in Table 2.2. The first point to be seen in the table is the general trend in both 1987 and 1994 for the wage ratio to fall over the age categories, in line with the fact that men's labour market careers tend to have fewer and shorter interruptions than women's. As regards a comparison of the 1987 and 1994 ratios, the most striking point to emerge is the rise in the female-to-male wage ratio in the younger age groups. For the youngest group, the gain is sufficiently strong that the hourly wages of these women now exceed the hourly wages of men in the same age group.[1] For the second youngest group, a small relative gain for women is also evident, although a gap still exists.

*Table 2.2: Average Hourly Earnings of Men and Women Classified by Age Category*

| Age Category | 1987 Ratio (%) | 1994 Ratio (%) | 1994 Male Hourly Wage | 1994 Female Hourly Wage |
|:---:|:---:|:---:|:---:|:---:|
| 15–24 | 93.2 | 107.9 | £3.94 | £4.25 |
| 25–34 | 92.8 | 95.1 | £7.00 | £6.66 |
| 35–44 | 85.6 | 81.5 | £8.97 | £7.31 |
| 45–54 | 77.8 | 71.5 | £9.90 | £7.08 |
| 55–64 | 95.0 | 76.6 | £9.90 | £7.58 |

The observation that younger women have earnings that are higher than their male counterparts gives rise to the question of whether this is a cohort effect (whereby the advantage will remain with these women as they get older) or whether it is an age effect (whereby the advantage will disappear as the women age and experience career interruptions). In order to address this question properly, it would be necessary to have information on individuals over time. However, it is important to keep this distinction in mind and not to assume that higher wages for younger women will necessarily persist as they age.

Women aged over 35 have experienced a decline in their average wage relative to men of the same age. As the wage ratio declines with age in both 1987 and 1994, the relative gain for younger women and the relative decline for older women between 1987 and 1994 imply that the age-related wage ratio decline has accelerated. This in turn implies that the age-related factors which reduce women's wages relative to men's have come to exert a greater influence on the relative earnings of men and women. This could be because of increased discrimination against older women relative to older men; however, it could also be due to

---

[1] The higher earnings of women relative to men in the youngest age group can be partly explained by their higher levels of education. While 79.1 per cent of these women have Leaving Certificates or higher, the corresponding figure for men is 62.1.

labour market experience and time out of the labour market (i.e. characteristics that are related to age) having become more important factors in determining wages. It could also be because of a changed composition of women workers at successive ages due to greater return to the labour market by women in mid-life. This issue will be addressed systematically in the following chapter.

Another factor which has been shown in many studies to affect the relative labour market outcomes of men and women is marriage and cohabitation. For this reason, in Table 2.3 we consider men and women living with partners (whether married or not) and singly; in addition, given the importance of age for wage ratios, we look at these sub-groups across different age categories. It should be noted that the 1987 figures referred to married people and others as opposed to "with partners" and others. Given the growth in the numbers cohabiting in recent years, we believe this classification is now more relevant.

*Table 2.3: Ratios of Female-to-Male Wages Classified by Age and Presence of Partner*

|  | 1987 Female-to-Male Ratio | | 1994 Female-to-Male Ratio | |
|---|---|---|---|---|
|  | *Partner* | *No Partner* | *Partner* | *No Partner* |
| 15–24 | too few | 95 | too few | 109.0 |
| 25–34 | 92 | 98 | 93.4 | 97.3 |
| 35–44 | 85 | 109 | 77.9 | 97.9 |
| 45–54 | 70 | too few | 69.1 | 96.0 |
| 55–64 | too few | too few | 71.3 | too few |

The first point to be taken from the table is that in both periods and across age categories, the ratios are higher for those with no partner/unmarried. This pattern is strongly related to labour market attachment, that is the greater likelihood of women interrupting their time in the labour force due to child-related issues. As women with partners are more likely to have children, they are also more likely to interrupt their careers and so to suffer a wage disadvantage relative to men of the same age. Given the difference between the two categories in terms of the size of the

wage ratio, we explore the wage differential for both groups separately in the following chapter.

Comparing particular cells across the two time periods, the
most striking feature is the relative gain for women with no partners in the youngest age category. Essentially, this is repeating the
finding on younger women generally from Table 2.2. If we look at
women with partners/married, we see a marginal relative gain in
the 25–34 age category, but relative declines in the 35–44 and 45–54
age categories. It could be that those in the 25–34 age group who
are with partners may not yet have had children. If this is so then
their relative gain, along with the relative decline for those over 35
and with partners, is consistent with a story based on the growing
importance of labour market experience and career interruptions.
While single women in the 35–44 age category are seen to have experienced a relative decline since 1987, the earlier figure is based
on less than 50 women, so care is required. Generally speaking, it
appears that the relative gain uncovered in Table 2.1 has been disproportionately accruing to younger, single women.

Given the importance of labour market experience generally in
the analysis, it is important to look at the wage differential across
experience categories. In Table 2.4, we categorise the sample of
employees by years of work experience. Given that the strongest
relative growth in female wage rates has been amongst the
youngest group, it is not surprising that the strongest relative
growth is also shown to have been occurring among the least experienced employees. A relative increase is also seen for those
with 15–25 years of experience while those in the 5–15 bracket
have essentially remained static. A big decline has occurred for
those in the 25–35 category.

While this last result is consistent with the relative decline for
older women seen above, the pattern in this table is not straight-
forward. Moving down the ratio columns, we see a relative increase, almost no change, another increase and a relative decline.
This pattern may be partly related to a difficulty with the measurement of experience in the survey. The total experience recorded for each person is the sum of all their periods in the labour
force. For some this could mean a few long periods (for most men
labour market experience would be one single period); for others,
their total experience could be made up of many short spells. Ei-

ther way, it is important to note the wage ratios within each of the experience categories are higher than the ratio based on all employees, i.e. 82 per cent. This would indicate that once we take time in the paid labour force into account, we can explain part of the overall wage difference.[2]

*Table 2.4: Average Hourly Earnings of Men and Women Classified by Length of Work Experience*

| Experience in Years | 1987 Ratio (%) | 1994 Ratio (%) | 1994 Male Hourly Wage | 1994 Female Hourly Wage |
|---|---|---|---|---|
| 0–5 | 93.9 | 109.3 | £4.05 | £4.43 |
| 5–15 | 87.1 | 86.5 | £6.74 | £5.83 |
| 15–25 | 83.8 | 89.6 | £8.84 | £7.92 |
| 25–35 | 104.9 | 95.4 | £9.79 | £9.34 |
| Over 35 | too few | 86.3 | £9.01 | £7.78* |

Education is an important wage determinant for men and women. Unlike experience, in which men usually have an advantage over women in terms of years worked, the years of education received by men and women are typically more similar. In the data being used here, women actually have higher levels of educational attainment. While equality in amounts of education received should reduce the gender wage gap, difference in rewards for additional years of education can add to gender wage differences. In Table 2.5, we consider this and look at wage ratios along the education dimension.

Looking down the ratio columns, we see in both years that the wage ratio is lower for lower levels of education. This is almost certainly due in part to greater differences in labour force attachment between men and women across education levels, as women with higher levels are less likely to interrupt their career for longer periods. As regards changes in the ratios between 1987 and 1994, the largest change has occurred among the group with Leaving Certificates and diplomas. The wage ratio for this group

---

[2] In the next chapter, we explore this more systematically by estimating separate wage equations for men and women, thereby allowing the "return" to experience to differ across the two groups.

has risen from 73.9 per cent to 80.5 per cent. For the other groups, the movements in the wage ratio have been small.

*Table 2.5: Average Hourly Earnings of Men and Women Classified by Level of Educational Attainment*

|  | 1987 Ratio (%) | 1994 Ratio (%) | 1994 Male Hourly Wage | 1994 Female Hourly Wage |
|---|---|---|---|---|
| No secondary qualifications | 68.7 | 65.8 | £5.96 | £3.92 |
| Group/Inter/Junior Cert | 70.2 | 73.2 | £6.23 | £4.56 |
| Leaving/post-leaving/diploma | 73.9 | 80.5 | £7.42 | £5.97 |
| University degree | 87.6 | 85.4 | £13.85 | £11.83 |

As women are concentrated into a limited number of occupations, the distribution of men and women across occupations may explain part of the overall wage gap. It could be that wage ratios in each occupational category are high but if women are more heavily concentrated in the lower-paid occupations, this will result in a smaller wage ratio across occupations. In order to investigate this we broke the sample into nine occupational categories. As there were too few observations in four of the categories on which to base a reliable estimate of the ratio, we only calculated the ratios for five categories and these are presented in Table 2.6.[3] In both time periods we find that the female/male wage ratio within each occupational category is lower than the overall wage ratio, except in the case of professional and technical workers. This tells us that the differences *within* groupings are more important than differences across groupings, at this broad level of occupational classification. It should not, however, be concluded from this that men and women are paid differently for doing the same job. Our data restricts us to looking at broad occupational classifications but it could be that men and women are distributed differently across jobs within each occupation. The conceptual and practical issues

---

[3] The omitted categories are agriculture, building and construction, transport and communication and a residual category of "other".

arising in using more detailed occupational classifications are considered in Chapter 4.

*Table 2.6: Average Hourly Earnings of Men and Women Classified by Occupation*

|  | 1987 Ratio (%) | 1994 Ratio (%) | 1994 Male Hourly Wage | 1994 Female Hourly Wage |
|---|---|---|---|---|
| Producers, makers and repairers | 71.3 | 73.3 | £6.40 | £4.69 |
| Clerical workers | 64.8 | 77.7 | £8.02 | £6.23 |
| Commerce, insurance and finance | 57.4 | 66.0 | £5.88 | £3.88 |
| Service workers | 57.9 | 57.5 | £6.63 | £3.81 |
| Professional and technical | 83.2 | 82.7 | £12.95 | £10.71 |

Focusing on the areas of greatest movement between 1987 and 1994, it can be seen that the largest relative gains have been made by clerical workers and by those working in commercial, insurance and finance occupations. Movements in relative wages in other occupations have been relatively minor. We return to sectoral issues in Chapter 4.

Our final breakdown of the male/female wage differential relates to part-time and full-time employment. Part-time employment is defined as less than 30 hours per week; but teachers working 24 hours or more are classified as full-time.

*Table 2.7: Average Hourly Earnings of Men and Women: Full-time and Part-time Employees*

|  | 1987 Ratio (%) | 1994 Ratio (%) | 1994 Male Hourly Wage | 1994 Female Hourly Wage |
|---|---|---|---|---|
| Full-time | 79.3 | 85.1 | £7.59 | £6.46 |
| Part-time | 70.4 | 58.0 | £10.72 | £6.22 |

We see that part-time women earn roughly the same average wage as full-time female employees; but the hourly wages of part-time men have risen very rapidly over the period. This phenomenon reflects not a rapid rise in the wage of the relatively small number of men working part-time in 1987, but an increase in part-time working among men in higher paid jobs, including teaching. It is this trend (still a limited one) towards increased part-time work by high-paid men which led to a sharp decline in the female-to-male wage ratio among part-time workers.

## 2.6 FROM 1994 TO 1997

In order to provide the most recent information possible on the female–male wage ratio, we draw on data from the 1997 version of the ESRI's *Living in Ireland Survey*. As with the 1994 version above, this is a nationally representative sample of households. The main focus of interest is on how the aggregate economy-wide wage gap has moved over a period of rapid labour market change.

Before looking at the value of the ratio in 1997, it is useful to consider key changes in the Irish labour market for the period 1994 to 1997. As a result of the economic boom, the labour market has experienced radical changes and it is possible that these changes will have impacted upon the gender wage differential in a number of different ways. Total employment (male and female) rose by 13 per cent or some 159,000; correspondingly, the unemployment rate fell sharply from close to 15 per cent to just above 10 per cent. Table 2.8 reports aggregates statistics on employment and unemployment for the years 1994 and 1997, broken down by gender.

*Table 2.8: Labour Market Statistics for the Years 1994 and 1997, by Gender*

|  | Men | | Women | |
|---|---|---|---|---|
|  | *1994* | *1997* | *1994* | *1997* |
| Employed (1,000s) | 766.3 | 840.3 | 454.3 | 539.7 |
| Unemployed (1,000s) | 131.9 | 97.1 | 79.1 | 62 |
| Economically active (1,000s) | 898.1 | 937.3 | 533.5 | 601.7 |
| Unemployment rate (%) | 14.7 | 10.4 | 14.8 | 10.3 |

*Source*: CSO (1997).

While the unemployment rates of the sexes have been remarkably similar over this three-year period, the percentage increase in employment has been substantially higher for women. Male employment increased by 74,000, or just under 10 per cent. Female employment increased by 85,400, or just under 19 per cent. Of this 85,400, 58,700 is an increase in full-time employment and 26,600 is an increase in part-time employment. Hence, although the percentage increase in part-time employment for women is larger than the percentage increase in full-time employment (27.1 per cent versus 16.5 per cent), the larger proportion of the total increase is made up of full-time employment.[4]

The fall in the number of unemployed women would suggest that some of the increase in employment has been facilitated by a movement from being unemployed to employed. However, an additional factor has been an increase in the female labour force participation rate between 1994 to 1997. In this period, the male participation rate was essentially static at around 68 per cent. The female participation rate rose from 39 per cent to 42 per cent. With about 1.4 million women aged over 15 in the population, this 3 per cent increase in participation translates into an extra 42,000 potential employees.

With such sizeable increases in female employment in the period 1994 to 1997, it is possible that the gender wage differential would be influenced by the composition of the employment increase — both in terms of the types of new jobs, and the characteristics of new employees. Increased participation by women returning to work, after long gaps in labour market experience can, in some circumstances, give rise to a fall in the female-to-male wage ratio. But greater attachment to the labour market through the childbearing and child-rearing years tends to raise the ratio. Were the new jobs for women largely well-paid, the female–male wage ratio would rise with the opposite holding if the new jobs were largely low-paid. Similarly, increases in participation among highly educated women would, other things being equal, tend to raise the ratio. Another factor that could influence the ratio is differences across occupations in wages changes, if such differences

---

[4] The numbers of full-time and part-time women in 1994 were 356,300 and 98,000 respectively; the corresponding number in 1997 were 415,000 and 124,600.

are correlated with differences in the gender make-up of occupations. With this in mind, we will present trends in earnings by occupation between the years 1994 and 1997, in Table 2.9.

**Table 2.9: Average Hourly Earnings of Full-time Employees in 1994 and 1997 and Real Annual Average Changes over the Same Period**

|  | 1994 £ | 1997 £ | Annual % Change, in Real Terms |
|---|---|---|---|
| Managers | 10.79 | 12.43 | 2.8 |
| Professional occupations | 11.96 | 13.08 | 1.0 |
| Associate professionals | 8.62 | 9.34 | 0.7 |
| Clerical occupations | 6.49 | 7.38 | 2.3 |
| Skill workers (maintenance) | 7.48 | 7.79 | −0.6 |
| Other skilled workers | 5.76 | 6.36 | 1.4 |
| Production operatives | 5.41 | 5.95 | 1.2 |
| Transport/communications | 5.76 | 6.69 | 3.0 |
| Sales workers | 4.61 | 5.78 | 5.7 |
| Security workers | 7.23 | 7.88 | 0.9 |
| Personal service workers | 4.18 | 5.40 | 6.8 |
| Labourers and others | 4.36 | 5.01 | 2.7 |
| Total | 7.13 | 8.07 | 2.2 |

*Source*: Sexton et al. (1999).

The numbers in the table are based on full-time employees in the 1997 *Living in Ireland Survey*. It can be seen that the biggest percentage increases were enjoyed by personal service workers and sales workers — occupations in which women tend to be highly represented — while the only fall was suffered by skilled workers (maintenance), a mainly male category. Such a pattern would suggest that that the changes in wages across occupations might have tended to raise the female-to-male wage ratio.

Only by providing an overall picture of the 1997 wage profile can the net impact of all these potentially conflicting factors be assessed. This is done using the *Living in Ireland* 1997 wave, which has recently become available for analysis.

    The net effect of the various changes is to produce a female–male wage ratio in 1997 of 84.5 per cent. This compares to a ratio of 82.4 per cent in 1994 and 80.1 per cent in 1987. Hence the trend observed earlier of an increased ratio between 1987 and 1994 has continued. As noted above, this change is the result of a mix of different forces, and further work would be require to disentangle the influences involved. One such analysis — designed to separate out the "explained" and "unexplained" components of the wage gap — is undertaken in the next chapter.

*Table 2.10: Average Hourly Earnings of Men and Women*

| | Female-to-Male Wage Ratio (%) | Hourly Wage | |
|---|---|---|---|
| | | *Men* | *Women* |
| *Living in Ireland, 1994* | 82.4 | £7.75 | £6.39 |
| *Living in Ireland, 1997* | 84.5 | £8.96 | £7.57 |

*Note:* The ESRI figures for 1997 are based on a total of 2,743 employees (1,563 men and 1,180 women). The figures reported above are weighted to ensure that they are representative of key characteristics of the population.

## 2.7 CONCLUSION

The principal findings of this chapter have been the relatively small increase in the economy-wide female/male wage ratio, from 80.1 per cent in 1987 to 82.4 per cent in 1994 and a continued increase to 84.5 per cent between 1994 and 1997. These gaps do not, however, make any adjustment for the labour-market-relevant characteristics of men and women (such as educational qualifications and length of labour market experience). In the next chapter, we will consider how the gap, adjusted for such characteristics, has evolved over the 1987 to 1994 and 1994 to 1997 periods.

    Wage ratio comparisons across subgroups in 1994 have shown relative declines for older women and relative increases for younger women. This is related to the higher educational qualifications of younger women relative to younger men, and may also be related to changes in the reward structure in the labour market, with an increased reward for experience in the paid labour market, and an increased penalty for time spent out of the paid labour market. If this were the case — an issue to be investigated in the next chapter — this could explain the observed pattern, as women will typically have experienced longer spells out of the workforce relative to men of the same age.

*Chapter 3*

# Decomposition of Wage Differentials

## 3.1 INTRODUCTION

We saw in the preceding chapter that male wages are higher on average than female wages. However, we also saw that the difference varies across subgroups and that in some cases female wages are actually higher than male wages. In this chapter, we analyse the male/female wage differential in a more systematic way. In particular, we decompose the difference in a way that will allow us to identify more precisely the sources of difference between the wages of men and women.

Two reasons can be mentioned for why such a decomposition is useful. Firstly, much of the discussion on male/female wage differences assumes that there is an element of discrimination against women involved in generating the difference. Although our decomposition technique does not allow us to measure discrimination precisely, it does allow us to isolate the component that is related to observable differences in the characteristics of male and female employees. As such, we can go some way towards estimating the extent to which the differential is related to women with the same characteristics as men being paid differently. The second reason for the decomposition relates to policy. In order to direct policy, it is useful to have an insight into the underlying causes of male–female wage differences. For example, if all or a substantial part of the wage difference could be attributed to differences in characteristics, then a policy aimed at reducing the gender wage gap would have to address the issue of why such differences in characteristics exist.

This chapter is structured as follows. In the next section, we will describe the methods used to decompose the wage difference and make some comments regarding their interpretation. We then go on to look at the results of the decompositions and compare them with the results which emerged from similar analyses conducted by Callan and Wren (1994) using the 1987 ESRI survey.

## 3.2 DECOMPOSITION METHODS

We begin this section by describing the decomposition methodology in an intuitive way. We go on to provide a more formal description later but the subsequent reporting of the results can be understood on the basis of the less formal description of the method which follows.

Consider a situation in which women and men enter the labour market with similar qualifications, and initially obtain the same wages. Now let us suppose that wages tend to rise with labour market experience (as is generally found to be the case in both national and international studies). Now let us consider some implications of a situation in which women who have children tend to withdraw from the labour force for a substantial period of time. This could lead to two factors tending to depress the wage of the average woman in the labour market relative to the average man. First, the average age of women in the labour market will tend to be lower than the age of the average man: employment rates for men would tend to be high and stable across all age groups, while employment rates for women would be highest for young women. Second, when women return from periods out of the labour market, they would tend to have less accumulated labour market experience than men of the same age.[1]

The standard approach to the decomposition of the gender wage gap begins by looking separately at male and female employees. For each of the two groups, relationships are estimated between wage rates and characteristics such as education and la-

---

[1] In some occupations, the lack of recent labour market experience could be particularly important; for example, in a fast-moving industry such as computing, skills might become out-of-date relatively quickly so that re-entrants to the labour market may find their earlier skills tend to lose value rather quickly. The data available to us at present are not sufficient to identify this effect.

bour market experience.[2] The estimated relationships show how these characteristics are rewarded for both men and women; for example, the relationship between wages and education shows how much extra an individual is paid for higher educational qualifications.

Given these estimates, we apply the male wage relationships to a theoretical woman whose characteristics are the average of all the women in the sample. In this way we calculate what an average woman would earn if her characteristics were rewarded in the same way as men's.[3] The difference between the average male wage and this constructed hypothetical female wage (based on male wage relationships) can be viewed as that part of the gender wage difference, which is due to differences in characteristics between men and women.

The difference between what an average woman earns and what she would earn if her characteristics were rewarded in the same way as men's cannot be explained by her characteristics; such a difference arises because her characteristics are rewarded differently than men's. This "unexplained residual" is often attributed to discrimination, although it could be due to other factors which have not been controlled for in the analysis. The residual can in turn be used to construct an index which has the following interpretation: it measures how much higher an average woman's hourly wage would be if her measured characteristics were rewarded in the labour market in the same way as men's.

This index is often referred to in the economics literature as the "discrimination index" but this is a rather imprecise usage, as the index cannot be regarded as either an upper or a lower bound to the true degree of discrimination. For this reason we follow Callan and Wren (1994) in calling it the "wage adjustment index". This latter term catches more precisely what the index actually measures; that is, the extent of the adjustment to the average woman's wage which, on the basis of the sample and control vari-

---

[2] The average characteristics of the men and women in the sample are shown in Table 3.5.

[3] While this theoretical woman may not exist in the sense that no individual woman in the sample has exactly the average collection of characteristics, "she" is nonetheless the most representative of the entire sample.

ables used, would arise if her characteristics were rewarded in the same way as men's. As a measure of the true extent of labour market discrimination, the index can be an over- or an underestimate.

To see why the index might underestimate labour market discrimination, consider the following. If direct discrimination in the labour market exists and women are paid less then men for certain characteristics, women may decide to invest less in education and to interrupt their careers more readily. Women will then be observed to have lower levels of human capital. In calculating the index, these human capital differences will form part of the wage gap that is "explained" and so will not be included in the measure of "discrimination". In this way, the index in a sense misses an element of labour market discrimination and so underestimates its true extent.

The potential for the index to overestimate the full extent of labour market discrimination can be understood through the following scenario. If women plan to interrupt their careers they may decide to invest less in on-the-job training and skill acquisition. If this is so, equal amounts of labour market experience will imply different levels of human capital accumulation for men and women. In this situation, men's experience will not represent equivalent human capital and so men may be more highly rewarded for each additional year in the labour market. This difference in returns to extra years of experience will be captured in the index and so will increase the measure of discrimination. However, the difference in returns to experience would not then be due to labour market discrimination and so the index would overstate the true extent of labour market discrimination.[4]

---

[4] It could be argued that discrimination makes it necessary for women to bear the burden of childcare and so be more likely to "choose" to interrupt their careers. While this may be true, this chapter only looks at discrimination that occurs in the labour market. In the situation where women are excluded from training, as opposed to choosing not to train, they will be observed to have lower earnings for the same level of experience, all else being equal. As such, this will be reflected in the wage adjustment index. Other explanations for unequal remuneration include different preferences, non-pecuniary benefits of work and different bargaining power, issues which are discussed below.

A further, and more general, difficulty arises in that our estimates of the relationships between wages and various characteristics leave much of the variation in wages unexplained. Datasets typically do not include information on all characteristics that might determine wages; some characteristics may not be observable while others may not have been recorded in the data. If any relevant characteristic is omitted from the data and its distribution differs across men and women, the wage adjustment index could be understating or overstating the true extent of labour market discrimination.

## A Formal Statement of the Decomposition Algebra

In order to clarify the discussion, and as an introduction to the econometric work that follows, we will now write out the wage equations (or relationships as we described them above) which we estimate for men and women below.

$$\log w_m = X_m B_m + e_m \tag{3-1}$$

$$\log w_f = X_f B_f + e_f \tag{3-2}$$

The w's are the wages of men and women (expressed in logarithmic form to ease interpretation later); the X's are vectors of characteristics (such as education and labour market experience); the B's are vectors of rewards or payments for the characteristics; and the e's are random error terms. These equations tell us that wages (those of males and females) are determined by characteristics, X, rewards, B, and some random component, e. Once we have estimated the equations using ordinary least squares regressions, the average wage difference between men and women can be written in the following form:

$$\overline{\log w_m} - \overline{\log w_f} = \beta_m (\overline{X_m} - \overline{X_f}) + (\beta_m - \beta_f)\overline{X_f} \tag{3-3}$$

A line over a quantity denotes that it is a mean value; we use Greek letters to denote estimated parameter values. As regressions estimated using ordinary least squares pass through the mean of the sample, it is possible to write the above equation and to omit any error terms. This equation is the basis for the standard approach to decomposing wage differences. The equation tells us again what was described intuitively above; the average wage differential (the left-hand side) can be split into two parts:

- Differences in average characteristics (the first component of the right-hand side) and

- Differences in rewards for those characteristics (the second component on the right-hand side).

As the last component captures the difference in average wages that cannot be explained by characteristics but instead are the result of differences in rewards for characteristics it is used, as we discussed above, to construct an index which is sometimes called the "discrimination index" but, for the reasons already given, we prefer to call it the "wage adjustment index". The index is constructed using the following formula:

$$D_f = 100(\exp(\beta_m - \beta_f)X_f - 1) \qquad\qquad (3\text{-}4)$$

Recalling that the dependent variable in the regressions is the logarithm of the hourly wage, $(\beta_m - \beta_f)X_f$ is a difference in logarithms and hence is equal to the logarithm of a quotient, that is, the logarithm of $\beta_m X_f/\beta_f X_f$. Taking the exponent of this logarithm gives average female wages, were they based on male returns, divided by average female wages. By subtracting one and multiplying by 100, we arrive at an index with the following interpretation: this index measures how much higher an average woman's wage would be if women's characteristics were rewarded at the same rates that men's characteristics are rewarded, i.e. if $\beta_f = \beta_m$.

What we have just outlined is known as the Oaxaca/Blinder approach to wage difference decomposition. In our analysis we employ a refinement of this standard approach which was used by Wright and Ermisch (1991). Possibly the single most important difference between the working lives of men and women is the greater propensity for women to spend time out of the labour force, due to childbearing and their generally more intensive role in child-rearing. In order to take account of this, Wright and Ermisch further decompose the wage differential in the following manner:

$$\overline{\log w_m} - \overline{\log w_f} = \beta_m (\overline{X}_m - \overline{X}_f) + (\beta_m - \beta_f)\overline{X}_f + (\alpha_m H_m - a_f H_f) \qquad (3\text{-}5)$$

where $\alpha = (\beta^{ynw}, \beta^{ynw^2})$

$$H = (\overline{ynw}, \overline{ynw}^2)$$

and $ynw$ = years not worked

It can be seen from the formula that the combined effects of time out of the workforce and the associated penalty (i.e. a negative reward) are subtracted and are not themselves decomposed. The reason for this (as discussed in Callan, 1991) is that the typical lengths of time out of the paid workforce are so different for men and women that the coefficients for one group are estimated over a range that differs substantially from the range of the other group. As such, the application of the coefficients of one group to the means of the other can produce misleading results.

## 3.3 ESTIMATED WAGE EQUATIONS AND RESULTS

In this section, we report estimates of the male and female wage equations as described in Equations (3-1) and (3-2) above. Although such estimates are very widely used in labour economics, there is some disagreement over what variables should be included as explanatory variables in the context of studies of male–female wage differentials. In particular, some argue that only variables which reflect elements of human capital should appear, such as education and experience; others argue that occupation should be included.

Here, we closely follow the specification used by Wright and Ermisch (1991). They discuss how they keep their specification simple so that the analysis focuses on differences in the coefficients of work experience and education. They omit occupational controls: as they point out, the inclusion of occupations as control variables "assumes that differences in occupational attainment are 'justified' but in fact they may be in part an outcome of discrimination" (p. 513). They argue that this simple specification leaves the focus on the "equal pay for equal human capital attributes" interpretation of discrimination.

By explicitly looking at time out of the workforce, the technique allows us to calculate the effect on women's pay relative to men's of such breaks, many of which will be taken for "caregiving" purposes. Not only is care-giving generally unrewarded in the labour market, in addition women are more likely to be penalised in the sense of their wages being lowered because of time out of the workforce. In spite of this advantage over the Blinder/Oaxaca approach, there remains the difficulty that productivity-increasing characteristics that are not observed in the data become part of the unexplained residual. This implies that if women have greater amounts of such unobserved characteristics, such as being good at teamwork, the wage adjustment index will be an understatement of the true extent of discrimination.

Given the different pattern of male/female wage ratios across people with and without partners (as shown in the previous chapter), we estimate wage equations and perform the decompositions for these two subgroups in addition to our analysis for the full sample. The data once again come from the ESRI's 1994 *Living in Ireland Survey*. In estimating the wage equations, we use the natural logarithm of the hourly gross wage. The questionnaire on which the dataset is based sought information on gross pay per period worked and hours worked. Combining these two, the hourly wage is derived; the logarithm is used, in common with most studies of this nature, as this eases the interpretation of the results and renders the distribution of errors more nearly normal.

We should note that our estimation approach differs in one respect from that of Wright and Ermisch. They adjusted for the sample selection using the Heckman correction technique; this adjusts the wage equations to account for the fact that not everyone in the population has an observed wage because some individuals do not have jobs, particularly women. As we do not perform this adjustment, our analyses are of differentials between the pay of those actually employed. We ignore any differences between the remuneration of those in work and that which would be offered to the non-employed were they to have jobs.

In Table 3.1, we present estimates of the wage equations for all male and all female employees. Looking firstly at the male coefficients, the pattern of results conforms to theoretical expectations. A positive coefficient on labour market experience (years worked in paid employment) and a negative coefficient on its squared value, implies that wages grow with experience, but at a decreasing rate. Higher levels of education are associated with higher wage levels. As described in the note to the table, the "returns" to each education category are measured relative to the omitted category of no secondary qualifications. Hence, the increase in coefficient size over the education categories is as expected. Urban areas are often associated with higher earnings and this is seen in the positive coefficient on the urban variable. The variable representing Dublin captures the wage effect of living in Dublin, above the urban effect captured by that variable; again, the Dublin coefficient is positive and significant. Having done an apprenticeship has a positive effect on wages but the estimate is not statistically significantly different from zero. Neither of the variables associated with unemployment rates is significantly different from zero. Finally, years out of the paid workforce lead to lower wages; a positive coefficient on the square of this variable implies that the negative effect increases with years out of the labour market but at a declining rate.

The equation for women follows a similar pattern, at least as regards the signs and significance of the variables. One exception is the sign of the apprenticeship coefficient which is negative for women, although insignificantly different from zero. The unemployment rate measures have large and significant negative coefficients. One possible interpretation is that high female unemployment causes lower female wages, but there may instead be a non-causative association between occupations and sectors with high rates of female unemployment and those with low pay.

*Table 3.1: Wage Equations for All Men and Women*

|  | Men | | Women | |
|---|---|---|---|---|
|  | *Coefficient* | *Standard Error* | *Coefficient* | *Standard Error* |
| Constant | .660 | .048 | 1.079 | .064 |
| Junior/Inter Cert.* | .210 | .032 | .086 | .042 |
| Leaving Cert.* | .381 | .034 | .259 | .041 |
| Diploma* | .559 | .046 | .430 | .053 |
| University degree* | .993 | .040 | .916 | .051 |
| Years worked | .068 | .003 | .062 | .004 |
| (Years Worked)$^2$ | −.001 | .0001 | −.001 | .0001 |
| Urban* | .113 | .024 | .054 | .026 |
| Dublin* | .060 | .026 | .051 | .028 |
| Completed apprenticeship* | .043 | .030 | −.031 | .081 |
| Unemployment rate in occupational group | −.026 | .142 | −.683 | .240 |
| Unemployment rate in industry | −.026 | .170 | −2.139 | .245 |
| Years out of paid work | −.016 | .007 | −0.014 | .004 |
| (Years out)$^2$ | .001 | .0003 | 0.0004 | .0001 |
|  | N = 1917 | Adj R$^2$ = .526 | N = 1390 | Adj R$^2$ = .542 |

*Note:* * indicates a dummy variable. Omitted categories are no educational quali-fication beyond primary, rural, non-Dublin, has not completed an apprentice-ship.

In Tables 3.2 and 3.3, we present the results for men and women with and without partners. The same pattern of results is broadly repeated. One puzzling element in the results is the negative coef-ficients on the unemployment variables in the male-with-partner equation and the positive coefficients in the male–without-partner equation. However, when the equations were run without these unemployment variables, their omission did not alter the overall pattern of results.

*Table 3.2: Wage Equations for Men and Women with Partners*

| | Men | | Women | |
|---|---|---|---|---|
| | *Coefficient* | *Standard Error* | *Coefficient* | *Standard Error* |
| Constant | 1.201 | .077 | 1.286 | .101 |
| Junior/Inter Cert.* | .170 | .034 | .078 | .052 |
| Leaving Cert.* | .378 | .037 | .295 | .052 |
| Diploma* | .543 | .052 | .492 | .069 |
| University degree* | .938 | .041 | .950 | .066 |
| Years worked | .041 | .005 | .038 | .007 |
| (Years Worked)$^2$ | −.001 | .0001 | −.001 | .0002 |
| Urban* | .022 | .027 | .042 | .035 |
| Dublin* | .086 | .028 | .052 | .039 |
| Completed apprenticeship* | .046 | .032 | −.004 | .126 |
| Unemployment rate in occupational group | −.517 | .177 | −.860 | .329 |
| Unemployment rate in industry | −.332 | .193 | −1.543 | .340 |
| Years out of paid work | −.040 | .008 | −.021 | .005 |
| (Years out)$^2$ | .002 | .0004 | .001 | .0002 |
| | N = 1175 | Adj R$^2$ = 0.471 | N = 757 | Adj R$^2$ = 0.531 |

*Note:* * indicates a dummy variable. Omitted categories are no educational qualification beyond primary, rural, non-Dublin, has not completed an apprenticeship.

We now turn to the decompositions of the wage differences, as described in the preceding section. The means on which these are based are presented in Table 3.5. In Table 3.4, we present both the Wright/Ermisch decompositions for the full sample and for the groups with and without partners; we also present the results from the 1987 data so that results can be compared and trends assessed.

*Table 3.3: Wage Equations for Men and Women without Partners*

|  | Men | | Women | |
|---|---|---|---|---|
|  | *Coefficient* | *Standard Error* | *Coefficient* | *Standard Error* |
| Constant | .558 | .084 | 1.147 | .094 |
| Junior/Inter Cert.* | .189 | .071 | .063 | .074 |
| Leaving Cert.* | .304 | .071 | .184 | .069 |
| Diploma* | .450 | .088 | .335 | .083 |
| University degree* | .902 | .087 | .823 | .081 |
| Years worked | .061 | .005 | .062 | .005 |
| (Years Worked)$^2$ | −.001 | .0001 | −.001 | .0002 |
| Urban* | .202 | .042 | .064 | .037 |
| Dublin* | .049 | .050 | .062 | .040 |
| Completed apprenticeship* | .063 | .057 | −.071 | .105 |
| Unemployment rate in occupational group | .422 | .224 | −.582 | .345 |
| Unemployment rate in industry | .341 | .295 | −2.687 | .348 |
| Years out of paid work | .031 | .014 | −.010 | .008 |
| (Years out)$^2$ | −.001 | .001 | .0001 | .0002 |
|  | N = 742 | Adj R$^2$ = .323 | N = 633 | Adj R$^2$ = .504 |

*Note:* * indicates a dummy variable. Omitted categories are no educational qualification beyond primary, rural, non-Dublin, has not completed an apprenticeship.

We begin by looking at the third column in Table 3.4, namely the components of the wage difference for the full sample in 1994. The first point to be made relates to a clarification on the observed wage gap. In the previous chapter, we established on the basis of our weighted sample that the national gender wage gap in 1994 was 82.4 per cent. The observed wage gap shown here relates to an unweighted sample; this is because the regressions on which the decompositions are based are run using the unweighted sample. Our interest here is not so much with the size of the wage differential but instead is with the proportion that can be attributed to years not worked (that is the length of time out of the workforce combined with the associated wage penalty), other characteristics and the residual.

*Table 3.4: Decomposition of Wage Gaps*

|  | All | | Partner | | No Partner | |
|---|---|---|---|---|---|---|
|  | *1987* | *1994* | *1987* | *1994* | *1987* | *1994* |
| Observed wage gap (logs) | 0.289 | 0.171 | 0.279 | 0.277 | 0.088 | −0.051 |
| *Of which % due to:* | | | | | | |
| Years not worked | 8.8 | 16.7 | 21.5 | 18.1 | −4.6 | −74.6 |
| Other attributes | 40.3 | 57.4 | 13.6 | 35.1 | −21.4 | 119.3 |
| Residual | 50.8 | 25.9 | 65.0 | 46.8 | 126 | 55.3 |
| $(\beta_m - \beta_f)\, \overline{X_f}$ | 0.147 | 0.044 | 0.181 | 0.129 | 0.112 | −0.028 |
| $D_f$ | 15.9 | 4.5 | 19.9 | 13.8 | 11.9 | −2.8 |

Over half of the gap between average male and female wages can be explained by differences in characteristics. Table 3.5 gives some insights into what produces this finding. The largest difference between the male and female means relates to labour market experience; in the sample, men have an average of 18 years of experience while women have an average of just under 12 years. A further 17 per cent of the wage gap can be explained by years out of the workforce. Again referring to Table 3.5, it can be seen that the average amount of time out of the workforce for women is close to five years as against less than one year for men.

Even when we take account of differences in characteristics between men and women and differences in the amount of time they spend out of the workforce, the unexplained residual still accounts for 25.9 per cent of the gap, which is .044 points out of the total gap of .171. Calculating the wage adjustment index as shown in Equation (3-4) above produces a value of 4.5 per cent; hence we can say that, based on our sample and the analysis we have performed, an average woman would earn almost 5 per cent more if her characteristics were rewarded in the same way as men's. As discussed in Chapter 2 above, this cannot be taken as a definitive upper or lower bound to the extent of discrimination.

*Table 3.5: Means for Men and Women used in Decompositions*

|  | All Males | All Females | Males with Partners | Females with Partners | Males without Partners | Females without Partners |
|---|---|---|---|---|---|---|
| Ln (Wage) | 1.82 | 1.65 | 2.07 | 1.79 | 1.42 | 1.47 |
| Junior/Inter Cert.* | 0.29 | 0.17 | 0.28 | 0.19 | 0.30 | 0.15 |
| Leaving Cert.* | 0.29 | 0.46 | 0.22 | 0.40 | 0.41 | 0.54 |
| Diploma* | 0.08 | 0.09 | 0.07 | 0.09 | 0.09 | 0.10 |
| University degree* | 0.14 | 0.15 | 0.16 | 0.15 | 0.10 | 0.14 |
| Years worked | 18.17 | 11.73 | 24.59 | 15.06 | 8.00 | 7.76 |
| (Years Worked)$^2$ | 498.25 | 218.96 | 715.10 | 290.99 | 154.85 | 132.82 |
| Urban* | 0.58 | 0.60 | 0.63 | 0.58 | 0.51 | 0.63 |
| Dublin* | 0.28 | 0.28 | 0.31 | 0.26 | 0.24 | 0.29 |
| Completed apprenticeship* | 0.14 | .02 | 0.15 | 0.01 | 0.11 | 0.03 |
| Unemployment rate in occupational group | 0.11 | 0.08 | 0.10 | 0.08 | 0.12 | 0.08 |
| Unemployment rate in industry | 0.10 | 0.08 | 0.09 | 0.08 | 0.11 | 0.09 |
| Years out of paid work | 0.93 | 4.80 | 1.01 | 7.21 | 0.79 | 1.91 |
| (Years out)$^2$ | 6.15 | 86.98 | 6.53 | 135.33 | 5.55 | 29.16 |
| N | 1,917 | 1,390 | 1,175 | 757 | 742 | 633 |

*Note:* * indicates a dummy variable: means then indicate the proportion of the group with the relevant attribute.

A question that naturally arises is whether these aggregate economy-wide results are evidence of payment practices which would contravene the current Employment Equality Act (1998), or its predecessors the Equal Pay Act and the Anti-Discrimination Act. As such laws are based on the principle of equal pay for the work of equal value *for the same employer*, there is still potential for unequal pay to emerge on an economy-wide basis because of the distribution of men and women across different employments. But even within employments, an "unexplained residual" of the type identified here might not constitute discrimination, if it was related to objectively justifiable factors not included in the equations estimated here.

Comparing the proportions in the third column of Table 3.4 with those in the second column gives a sense of how the components of the gender wage gap have changed relative to each other between 1987 and 1994. The wage adjustment index fell substantially over this period. While the average woman in 1987 would have earned almost 16 per cent more if her characteristics had been rewarded in the same way as men's, by 1994 the corresponding figure had fallen to 4.5 per cent. A similar picture emerges if we compare the proportions of the wage gap that are due to the "unexplained residual" in 1987 and 1994; the proportion fell from 51 per cent to 26 per cent. To the extent that the wage adjustment index does measure discrimination, these figures would indicate that discrimination has fallen. However, we make that statement mindful of the limitations inherent in the index as a measure of discrimination.

The wage adjustment index for women living with partners also falls, from 20 per cent to 14 per cent. The pattern of change for this group differs from the full sample in that years not worked has become relatively less important as a component of the gender wage differential. Other characteristics have become relatively more important, rising from 14 per cent of the differential to 35 per cent. While the proportion of the differential that is the unexplained residual has fallen from 65 per cent to 47 per cent, the decline is less than in the case of the full sample.

The figures in Table 3.4 which relate to those not living with partners in 1994 require a small clarification. As the female wage is larger than the male wage for this group and so the wage difference is negative, a positive percentage (such as the 55 per cent which is attributed to the unexplained residual) arises when the value of the component was also negative (such as the –0.28 value for the unexplained residual). Given that the unexplained residual is negative, the wage adjustment index is also negative. The interpretation of the figure for this group is therefore that the average woman (without a partner) would earn 2.8 per cent *less* if her characteristics were rewarded in the same way as men's.

As with the full sample and the group with partners, the decompositions indicate that the unexplained residual is putting women at a disadvantage to a lesser degree in 1994 than in 1987. The change for the group who are not living with partners is such that the unexplained residual is now giving women an advantage.

### 3.4 DECOMPOSITION FOR 1997

In Chapter 2, we observed that the female–male wage ratio rose again between 1994 and 1997. We will now use the same decomposition methodology to see if the structure of the gender wage gap has changed in this period. As described in Chapter 2, the large increase in female employment leaves open the possibility that the small change in the size of the wage differential between 1994 and 1997 may be the result of offsetting structural changes.

In Table 3.6, we present the log wage gap for the same three groups (all cases, those with partner, and those without partner) in 1997 and the percentage breakdown across the components, just as we did in Table 3.4 for the years 1987 and 1994. We also show the wage-adjustment index.

*Table 3.6: Decomposition of Wage Gaps, 1997*

|  | All | With Partner | Without Partner |
|---|---|---|---|
| Observed wage gap (logs) | .198 | .325 | −0.043 |
| *Of which % due to:* |  |  |  |
| Years not worked | 18 | 18.7 | −37.5 |
| Other attributes | 52.9 | 41.1 | 159.4 |
| Residual | 29.1 | 40.3 | −21.8 |
| $(\beta_m - \beta_f) X_f$ | 0.057 | 0.130 | 0.008 |
| $D_f$ | 5.8 | 13.9 | 0.8 |

We note at the outset that the observed logarithmic wage gap for 1997 is slightly larger than that for 1994, contrasting with the fall in the gender wage gap seen over the same period in Chapter 2.

There are a number of technical reasons for this,[5] but for the present our main focus is on the *structure* of the wage gaps in 1994 and 1997 rather than a direct comparison of the wage gaps for the two years. Our interest at this point is not so much in the size of the gap but rather in the structure and how this compares to the structure in 1994. Looking at the column for all employees, it can be seen that the structure is very similar to what it was in 1994. In 1994, 17 per cent of the wage difference was due to time out of the labour force; in 1997, this figure was 18 per cent. Another 57 per cent of the difference in 1994 could be explained by other attributes; the corresponding figure was 53 per cent in 1997. Finally, the unexplained residual made up 26 per cent of the wage gap in 1994; in 1997, the unexplained residual amounted to 29 per cent.

A similar pattern is also observed for the "with partner" group. The percentages in Table 3.6 match closely those in Table 3.4. For the "no partner" group, the percentages are rather different; but it should be remembered that the gap for this group is much smaller and so any changes in the components of the gap are magnified when we view them in percentage terms.

The broad picture suggested by our analysis is that the "unexplained" gender wage gap fell quite sharply over the 1987 to 1994 period, but was more stable between 1994 and 1997. The estimated overall "wage adjustment index" in 1997 was just below 6 per cent, with a low value (less than 1 per cent in 1997) for women without partners and a higher value (14 per cent) for women with partners.

## 3.5 CONCLUSION

Our purpose in this chapter has been to systematically decompose the gender wage gap and to attribute it to three components — years not worked, other characteristics and an unexplained residual which arises because men and women receive different re-

---

[5] Briefly, these consist of the fact that the mean of the logarithms is a geometric mean (required for the decomposition algebra), as against the more familiar arithmetic mean; a certain reduction in the number of cases available for the econometric analysis, due to missing information on a subset of variables; and the use of unweighted analyses in the regressions and associated decompositions, as against weighted analyses for the descriptive analyses of Chapter 2.

wards for their characteristics. We then calculated an index based on the unexplained residual which tells how much higher the average woman's wage would be if her characteristics were rewarded in the same way as men's. While some describe this index as a "discrimination index", we prefer to use the more precise term the "wage adjustment index" as there are reasons to believe that the index can either understate or overstate the true extent of labour market discrimination.

The results for all employees in 1994 show that the "wage adjustment index" had a value of almost 5 per cent; this would imply that an average woman, were her characteristics to be rewarded in the same way as men's, would earn almost 5 per cent more than her actual earnings. The corresponding value in 1997 was similar at 5.8 percent. This represents a considerable reduction from the corresponding 1987 figure of close to 16 per cent. The index has also fallen between 1987 and the mid-1990s for both people living with partners and those not living with partners.

Referring back to the previous chapter, it will be remembered that the female/male wage ratio rose by 2.3 percentage points between 1987 and 1994. While this is not a very large change, the fall in the wage adjustment index from about 16 per cent to almost 5 per cent points to more substantial changes in the underlying determinants of male and female wages. In 1987, about half of the gender wage gap was due to differences in characteristics and time out of the paid workforce; in 1994 and in 1997, around three-quarters of the gap can be attributed to these factors.

The findings of a small increase in the female/male wage ratio and a somewhat larger reduction in the wage adjustment index may be partly explained by the increase in female labour force participation in recent years. If the skills of the new female entrants/re-entrants are lower on average than the existing pool of female employees, the female/male wage ratio would fall, all else being equal.

The female employees in the 1994 data have spent, on average, 4.8 years out of the paid workforce. The corresponding figure for the 1987 data was 3.9 years. At the same time, there was a small fall (0.9 years to 0.8 years) in time spent out of the paid workforce for men. This would, given the negative impact of time spent out of the labour market, tend to increase the gender wage gap. On the other hand, female employees in 1994 had longer work experience than in 1987 (11.7 as against 10.4 years) while male employees in 1994 had somewhat less experience than in 1987 (18.2 years as against 19.6), tending to reduce the observed gap.

Another element explaining the conjunction of a small rise in the observed female/male wage ratio and a larger fall in the wage adjustment index is that there have been changes in the reward structure in the labour market (specifically, the returns to labour market experience and the penalty attached to time spent out of the paid workforce) which have tended to reduce the female/ male wage ratio. This point is taken up in more depth in Chapter 6.

*Chapter 4*

# Measuring and Explaining the Wage Gap: Some Broader Issues

## 4.1 INTRODUCTION

In the previous two chapters, our analysis of the difference in labour market outcomes for male and female employees has focused on hourly wage rates. In this chapter, we will broaden our analysis and consider differences between male and female employees in their receipt of fringe benefits. While looking at fringe benefits broadens our analysis, our interest in them is closely linked to the wage analysis of the previous two chapters. In essence we want to know if differences in receipt of fringe benefits add to or subtract from the observed gap in gross wages, to create a greater or lesser gap in "total compensation" between the sexes.

Much of the report has been concerned with measuring and decomposing the male/female wage differential. In particular, we have been interested in establishing the degree to which the differential can be explained by differences between the sexes in productivity-related characteristics such as education and experience. While we have found that some of the differential can be explained in this way, there still exists an unexplained component that may be the result of discrimination.

In this chapter we discuss further some of the broad conceptual issues surrounding male–female wage differentials. One issue we will focus on is the extent to which the gender wage gap can be explained in terms of the distribution of men and women across different occupations and sectors. The exploration of these conceptual issues can help not only in the interpretation of results presented in previous chapters, but also to guide strategies for future research. We have noted already that sample sizes impose limitations on the degree of occupational disaggregation which can be used in the analysis. As there are only small numbers of individuals in certain occupational and sectoral cells once a sufficiently fine classification is used, it is not possible to draw reliable conclusions about gender wage differentials within these cells. One response to this problem is to seek to increase sample sizes substantially. On the basis of the conceptual discussion that follows, we will argue that there may be more efficient ways to explore the issues of interest.

The chapter is structured as follows. In the next section we examine the incidence of fringe benefits. Section 4.3 discusses the main theories in the economics literature which have been used to explain the gender wage differentials and occupational segregation. Section 4.4 reviews empirical studies of the relationship between the gender wage gap and the distribution of the sexes across occupations. We report on Irish studies that have calculated the degree of occupational segregation in the Irish labour market. Section 4.5 outlines the limitations of existing data for the analysis of some of the issues raised. Section 4.6 makes some suggestions as to how the issues might be examined in future. The main findings and conclusions are drawn together in the final section.

## 4.2 INCIDENCE OF FRINGE BENEFITS

In order to gain some insights into the receipt of fringe benefits, we once again draw on the 1994 *Living in Ireland Survey*, described in Chapter 2. On the individual questionnaires, people with jobs were asked a number of questions about whether their employer offered certain benefits to employees and whether the individuals themselves benefited. One of these questions asked if the person would be entitled to a pension from their work on retirement; as this fringe benefit typically has the largest monetary value, differences in pension entitlements are of particular interest. Another question asked if the individual benefited from the free or subsidised provision by the employer of the following services: child minding facilities; health care or medical insurance; education and training; sports and leisure/holiday centre; housing/reduced mortgages. Ideally we would like to use the monetary value of the fringe benefits and to calculate a total compensation measure. However, it would be extremely difficult to obtain such information from individual employees; for example, many young or middle-aged workers covered by pension schemes would not be able to provide detailed information on their future pension benefits in a way which would allow such quantification. Thus, the survey data do not contain this information and so we can only assess the different incidence of these benefits across men and women.

In Table 4.1, we show what proportions of men and women responded that they would be entitled to a pension from work; we also show the proportions who responded that they benefited from the employers' provision of the services mentioned above. Looking firstly at pensions, we see that while 53.7 per cent of male employees have job-related pension entitlements, only 38 per cent of female employees had the same entitlement. If we think of the reward from work being a combination of pay now and a pension paid upon retirement, then this difference in pension entitlement clearly adds to the pay gap shown in Chapters 2 and 3.

*Table 4.1: Proportions of Male and Female Employees who Benefit from Various Fringe Benefits*

|  | Males (%) | Females (%) |
| --- | --- | --- |
| Pension | 53.7 | 38.0 |
| Childcare | 0.2 | 0.4 |
| Health/Medical insurance | 16.2 | 7.2 |
| Education/Training | 20.9 | 20.4 |
| Sport/Leisure | 11.5 | 7.3 |
| Housing/Mortgage | 3.2 | 1.5 |

Turning to other fringe benefits, we can see that male employees are more likely to receive health and medical insurance benefits, free or subsidised sport and leisure, and housing or mortgage benefits. This will tend to add further to the gap in "total compensation" between men and women.

There is little difference between the incidence of ongoing education and training provided by employers to employees. This is of particular significance because a greater incidence for men would have provided an indication that the men in the sample could have expected faster wage growth in subsequent years, thus adding to the wage differential. While the incidence of training is similar for men and women, there may, of course, be differences in the intensity or quality of training provided: the data gathered in the *Living in Ireland Survey* were not designed to address this issues.

Female employees are more likely than men to benefit from free or subsidised childcare facilities, but the incidence of this benefit is by far the lowest for both sexes. While it may be of particular significance to the individuals concerned, it would have little impact on the aggregate compensation differences between the sexes.

Just as wage rates are partly determined by the characteristics of the employee, so also is the likelihood of receiving fringe benefits related to employee characteristics. For example, better educated workers typically have better "quality" jobs, where higher wages are accompanied by fringe benefits. For this reason, we need to explore if the difference in the likelihood of male and female employees receiving benefits is a result of differences in their characteristics. In order to do this, we estimate functions that relate individual characteristics to the likelihood of receiving benefits. By including male and female employees in the regressions and estimating the coefficient for being male as opposed to female, we can say that we are estimating the impact of being male on the likelihood of receiving benefits, controlling for other characteristics.

As our dependent variable only takes values of 0 or 1 (i.e. the individual receives the benefit or not), it would be inappropriate to use the ordinary least squares (OLS) regression technique which was used in Chapter 2. Instead, we estimate probit models; such models employ a functional form that takes account of the probabilistic nature of the relationships that we are estimating. In particular, rather than fitting a linear relationship between the dependent and independent variables, a probit regression fits a cumulative normal distribution. In this way, predicted values of the dependent variable are constrained to lie between zero and one. This is consistent with the predicted values of the dependent variable being probabilities. Were an OLS linear regression to be fitted it is possible that predicted values of the dependent variable would lie outside the zero–one range.

We report on two sets of models: in Table 4.2, we report on the results when occupational categories are not included as controls while in Table 4.3 we show the results which emerged from regressions with occupational controls. A comparison of the two sets of models will help us to address if differences in receipt of benefits across the sexes is simply related to the different occupations held by the two groups. Given the very small numbers who receive childcare and housing/mortgage benefits, probit models are not estimated for them.

The model relating characteristics to whether or not a pension is received shows a pattern of coefficients that would be expected. Longer experience is associated with a greater likelihood of pension entitlements while time out of the workforce reduces this likelihood. The likelihood of entitlement rises with education and is also higher for urban dwellers. As regards male and female employees, the coefficient on the sex dummy variable indicates that male employees are more likely to be entitled to a pension, even when we control for these other characteristics. Hence, the difference shown in Table 4.1 in the proportions of male and female employees who have work-related pension entitlements cannot be explained away by differences in characteristics.

The pattern of results on the health model is very similar to that of the pensions model, which is not surprising. Again, there remains a statistically significant difference between men and women even when we control for the other characteristics. The lack of a difference between men and women as regards training and education which was seen in the means in Table 4.1 is reflected in the lack of statistical significance on the sex dummy variable in the education/training model. The positive and significant coefficient on the sex dummy variable in the sport/leisure model again indicates a male advantage in terms of the probability of receiving such benefits.

*Table 4.2: Results from Probit Regressions Estimating Likelihood of Being in Receipt of the Benefits Mentioned[1]*

| | Pensions | | Health | | Education/Training | | Sport/Leisure | |
|---|---|---|---|---|---|---|---|---|
| | Coefficient | z | Coefficient | Z | Coefficient | Z | Coefficient | Z |
| Years worked | 0.141 | 19.827 | 0.050 | 5.935 | 0.037 | 4.959 | 0.030 | 3.296 |
| (Years worked)$^2$ | -0.002 | -13.202 | -0.001 | -4.599 | -0.001 | -4.789 | -0.001 | -3.382 |
| Years out of paid workforce | -0.103 | -8.508 | -0.063 | -3.501 | -0.061 | -4.241 | -0.036 | -1.373 |
| (Years out)$^2$ | 0.003 | 5.877 | 0.001 | 1.900 | 0.001 | 2.199 | -0.001 | -0.647 |
| Urban | 0.236 | 3.995 | 0.314 | 4.421 | 0.295 | 4.777 | 0.325 | 4.257 |
| Dublin | 0.110 | 1.717 | 0.079 | 1.091 | 0.095 | 1.478 | 0.142 | 1.884 |
| Group/Inter/Junior Cert | 0.064 | 0.753 | 0.170 | 1.632 | 0.364 | 3.529 | 0.155 | 1.350 |
| Leaving Cert | 0.516 | 6.031 | 0.285 | 2.751 | 0.590 | 5.874 | 0.163 | 1.429 |
| Diploma | 0.719 | 6.414 | 0.381 | 2.933 | 0.918 | 7.688 | 0.218 | 1.529 |
| University | 1.181 | 11.615 | 0.220 | 1.920 | 0.876 | 8.168 | 0.241 | 1.945 |
| Sex (male) | 0.120 | 2.138 | 0.350 | 5.072 | -0.004 | -0.074 | 0.170 | 2.408 |
| Constant | -1.979 | -17.670 | -2.189 | -16.113 | -1.721 | -14.246 | -1.910 | -13.425 |
| | N = 3274 | | N = 3305 | | N = 3305 | | N = 3305 | |
| | Log likelihood = -1700.6376 | | Log likelihood = -1150.8569 | | Log likelihood = -1556.6348 | | Log likelihood = -1001.8461 | |

[1] The z statistic, like the t statistic in the OLS models of Chapter 3, indicate the degree of statistical significance of the coefficient estimate. Absolute values greater than 1.96 indicate significance at the 95 per cent confidence level.

In Table 4.3, we show the coefficients on the sex dummy variables when the probit models include occupational controls. The pattern of results in terms of signs and significance is essentially the same across the two tables. We do, however, see a large increase in the size of the sex dummy variable coefficient relating to pensions. This would indicate that differences *within* occupations between male and female employees in terms of their receipt of pension benefits are significant.

*Table 4.3: Coefficients on the Sex Dummy Variable in Probit Regressions Controlling for Occupational Categories*

|  | Coefficient on Sex Dummy Variable | Z Statistic |
|---|---|---|
| Pensions | 0.224 | 3.485 |
| Health | 0.322 | 4.233 |
| Education/training | 0.042 | 0.661 |
| Sport/leisure | 0.145 | 1.845 |

Although our data do not contain information on the value of fringe benefits, we can at least impute values for two of the benefits and thereby produce estimates of how the inclusion of fringe benefits impacts upon the female–male wage ratios. In the case of pensions we do this in the following way. For those who are covered by pension benefits, we examine the impact of adding 5 per cent or 10 per cent to hourly wages on the assumption that employers pay something in that range as pension contributions. We then re-calculate the wage ratios using weights as described in Chapter 2.

We also add an estimate of the value of health benefits. Assuming health benefits cost £300 per year and that people work 48 weeks per year, this amounts to a weekly benefit of £6.25. For those in receipt of health benefits, we divide £6.25 by the number of hours they usually work in a week. This gives us an hourly value of health benefits that can be added to the hourly wage. We add this to our estimates of hourly wages, inclusive of the 10 per cent pension contribution, and again re-calculate the wage ratios. The results are presented in Table 4.4

*Table 4.4: Female-to-Male Wage Ratios Including Imputed Values for Employers' Pension Contributions and Health Benefits*

| Wage Ratio | Wage Plus 5% Pension | Wage Plus 10% Pension | Wage Plus 10% Pension Plus Health Benefit |
|:---:|:---:|:---:|:---:|
| 82.4 | 81.6 | 81 | 80.8 |

We saw in Tables 4.1 and 4.2 that men were more likely to receive pension benefits and health benefits than women and this is reflected in Table 4.4. The inclusion of imputed values for the benefits reduces the wage ratio. The impact of pensions on the ratio is larger than that of health benefits because, under our assumptions and most likely in reality, pensions are considerably more valuable. While a 10 per cent pension contribution increases the average hourly wage by 60 pence for men and 38 pence for women, the corresponding values for health benefits are only 3 pence and 2 pence.

### 4.3 THEORIES EXPLAINING THE GENDER WAGE DIFFERENTIAL AND OCCUPATIONAL SEGREGATION

Within the economics literature, there are three broad theories that have been used to explain the relative labour market outcomes of different groups. The theories were mostly developed in the context of racial differences in the US but can be readily applied to gender differences. We will consider each of the three in turn.[2]

### 4.3.1 Taste-based Discrimination

This theory was originated by Becker (1957) and is a useful tool for translating the concept of prejudice into an economic framework. The discrimination involved may be on the part of employers, employees or customers, but we begin by considering the theory in the context of *discrimination by employers*. Suppose that women earn a wage $w_w$. If an employer does not like employing women, the utility-adjusted cost to him of hiring a woman is

---

[2] Most of the discussion in this section is drawn from Borjas (1996).

greater than $w_w$. We can say that the cost to the prejudiced employer of hiring a woman is $w_w \times (1+d)$, where d is the discrimination coefficient. For a non-prejudiced employer, d is equal to zero. For a prejudiced employer d is greater than zero and it increases as the degree of prejudice increases.

Viewing discrimination in this way produces strong hypotheses about the subsequent structure of employment. Suppose that men and women are equally productive. A non-prejudiced employer (i.e. d = 0) will hire whichever workers are cheaper. If female wages are below male wages, such an employer will only hire women. Employers who are slightly prejudiced may also hire women only. If their d is sufficiently small, the utility-adjusted cost of hiring a woman [$w_w \times (1+d)$] may still be less than the male wage. However, once d is sufficiently large, $w_w \times (1+d)$ will exceed the male wage and only men will be hired. As such, under the restrictive assumptions imposed, employment will be completely segregated along sex lines.

The theory also predicts that women's wages will be below those of men. Suppose men's and women's wages are initially equal. All prejudiced firms will only hire men. This demand for male workers and lack of demand for female workers will tend to induce an increase in male wages and a fall in female wages. As the ratio of female to male wages falls, some slightly prejudiced employers will be prepared to hire women. Eventually an equilibrium will be reached in which male wages are above those of female wages.

While this theory is both simple and useful in terms of understanding how discrimination can manifest itself in the labour market, it is not without internal contradictions. Given that prejudiced employers hire men as opposed to women, their wage bill is higher than it need be and they employ fewer workers than is optimal. If all firms face the same production functions, the implication for the prejudiced employers is that they should be forced out of business. Non-prejudiced employers will be able to produce goods more cheaply and will undercut the prejudiced employers. In this way market forces should eliminate prejudiced employers. As male–female and other forms of wage differentials persist, this market-led eradication of discrimination seems unlikely. In order for the persistence of discrimination to be consistent with the

Becker model, some additional assumptions are required whereby prejudiced employers have either lower costs of production or some form of monopoly power.

Our discussion so far has only looked at discrimination on the part of employers. The theory can be extended to include discrimination on the part of other employees and consumers. In the case of *discrimination by employees*, suppose men do not like working with women and women are indifferent between working with men or other women. If a man is to take a job in an integrated firm he will discount the value of his wage to take account of the disutility associated with working with women. His utility adjusted wage will be $w_m \times (1-d)$, where d is now the male employee's discrimination coefficient. If an integrated firm is to hire a male, they will have to offer him higher wages to compensate for the presence of women.

Like the employer model of discrimination, the employee model leads to the prediction that the labour market will be completely segregated along sex lines. An integrated firm will have to pay higher wages to compensate males; such payments can be avoided by employing only members of one sex. As competitive pressures will drive out firms that do not minimise costs, any integrated firms will cease to exist. Unlike the employer model, the employee model does not lead to a prediction that a wage differential will exist across firms. Once men and women are employed in separate firms there is no need to pay them differently and any pay differences would be erased by competitive pressures.

*Consumer discrimination* arises when people purchasing goods or services have a preference for dealing with men rather than women. If the price of the good or service is p, the prejudiced consumer will act as if the price is $p \times (1+d)$ where d is now the consumer's discrimination coefficient. The effect of the discrimination in this case will depend on the nature of the establishment. If women can be moved to jobs within the firm that do not involve contact with consumers, occupational segregation will be generated although a wage differential is not necessarily implied. If it is not possible to move women away from contact with consumers, then employers will have to reduce prices to compensate consumers and this will in turn become reflected in female wages relative to male wages.

### 4.3.2 Statistical Discrimination

The crucial distinction between taste-based discrimination and statistical discrimination is that the latter does not involve a dislike for women or ethnic minorities. Instead, the less favourable treatment of women arises because employers believe that the information they use to predict an individual's true productive capacity is less reliable for women then for men.

The theory is most easily illustrated through an example. Suppose two individuals apply for a job. Their curriculum vitaes are identical and they perform equally well in interviews. One of the individuals is a man while the other is a woman. While the company believes that there is a correlation between the information they gather on individuals and their productive capacity, the correlation is not perfect. They need to supplement the information on the individual with additional facts. The information they use may be based on the average characteristics of the group to which the individuals belong. In this example, the company will calculate that women on average are more likely to quit than men. As a result, they offer her a lower wage relative to an equally qualified man.

While such a scenario may appear to imply discrimination against women, it actually implies discrimination against some women only. In addition, it implies positive discrimination against other women. By basing judgements of potential productivity on the group average, women who would remain with the firm are discriminated against. However, women who would have left even earlier than the group average would be paid more than their true productivity may warrant. On average, women as a group will not be discriminated against under this scenario.

Discriminatory outcomes can arise from information difficulties of the sort just discussed. If employers want to avoid risk and if the information about women is considered less reliable than that for men, the employer may pay a women less in compensation for the greater perceived risk associated with her hiring. In this situation, all women will be paid less.

From a policy perspective, statistical discrimination raises difficulties. While it may generate unfavourable outcomes for women in the labour market it is not easy to see how such behaviour can be avoided. Profit-maximising firms will always want to ensure that their hiring decisions use all the information available to them. In the absence of perfect information on employees, risk-averse employers will look to be compensated for risk and if they are more unsure of women's future productivity, they may pay women less. Such "statistical discrimination" would seem to be outlawed by the Employment Equality Act; but if so, its enforcement would also have to be based on statistical information and analysis, rather than a case-by-case approach.

### 4.3.3 Occupational Segregation

While this category of theories sees the different labour market outcomes of men and women as being the result a process whereby each gender is directed into certain occupations, the underlying processes differ. We will present two stories and show how each scenario leads to higher wages for men relative to women. Our choice of stories is motivated by a desire to demonstrate two competing theories, both of which are consistent with higher concentrations of women in some occupations and lower relative wages for women. The theories differ, however, in terms of how they perceive the source of the segregation and hence what policies they imply.

We will call the first theory "demand-generated occupational segregation". Under this theory, certain jobs are only open to men. All other jobs are open to men and women. The result of this is that the supply of women to these latter jobs is increased. If wages are set according to the laws of supply and demand, the restricted supply of labour in the men-only jobs raises wages. In contrast, the increased supply to the jobs that are open to all reduces wages. The overall result is higher relative wages in the men-only jobs and lower relative wages in the other jobs that will be dominated by women.

In the scenario just outlined, the segregation arises because women's choices are restricted. In an alternative view of occupational segregation, the different concentrations of men and women across occupations arises because of the choices made by women. We will label this "supply-generated occupational segregation". Suppose women want to have greater freedom and flexibility regarding their hours of work. If this is so, they may choose jobs that provide such flexibility but which pay lower wages as a result. In the language of labour economics, the jobs done mainly by men offer a "compensating differential" in respect of the reduced flexibility. The net result is that the jobs done mainly by women will be observed to pay less, even when productivity-related characteristics are taken into account.

While we have discussed this second scenario using the term "choices", it could be that the labour market "choices" of women are strongly influenced by circumstances outside of the labour market.[3] In particular, if the burden of home duties falls on women, they may require greater flexibility in their jobs. While this may be symptomatic of a form of discrimination, the discrimination is not happening in the labour market. As such, policies to reduce the occupational segregation that arises from the supply-side must take account of the source of the segregation. Policies that promote equal opportunities will have little effect if women are "choosing" not to enter certain occupations. In contrast, such policies will have an impact if the occupational segregation is demand-generated.

This review of the theories illustrates an important point about the relationship between the gender wage differential and occupational segregation. In the case of taste-based and statistical discrimination, occupational segregation is generated along with the wage difference but it is not the source of the wage difference. In the case of demand-generated occupational segregation, the segregation does cause the wage gap. Supply-generated occupational segregation also leads to a wage differential but the source of the differential is choices made by women. In summary, the relationship between occupational segregation and the gender wage gap is complex. By extension, policies which seek to reduce the gender wage gap through reducing occupational segregation will only be successful if the nature of the segregation is understood. For example, if taste-based discrimination on the part of employers prevents women from receiving the training that facilitates

---

[3] Relevant factors could include school structures influencing subject choices, or the lack of role models in certain professions and occupations, which could in part be due to a legacy of past discrimination.

promotion, policies to provide childcare or more flexible working arrangements may have little impact on segregation. In this case, affirmative action measures may be required.

## 4.4 EMPIRICAL STUDIES ON OCCUPATIONAL SEGREGATION AND THE GENDER WAGE DIFFERENTIAL

When undertaking the Oaxaca-type decompositions of the gender wage differential, the issue arises of whether or not to include occupation as an explanatory variable. If occupation is included and the classification is sufficiently fine, a large amount of the "unexplained" gap will be explained. Gunderson (1989), noted when writing about the US, Canada and Britain that "pay differences for the same narrowly defined occupation within the same establishment [do] not account for much of the [male–female] gap". For this reason, inclusion of narrowly defined occupations in the wage equations will make it look as if the wage gap is due to the different productive characteristics of men and women and the different jobs that they do. However, if the distribution of men and women across occupations is due to discrimination, then it is somewhat misleading to include occupation in the wage equations and to treat the gendered distribution of occupations as being justified.

One study of the link between occupational segregation and the gender wage gap in Ireland is Callan (1991). Wage equations were estimated using data from the 1987 ESRI large-scale household survey; ten occupational categories were included. The results suggested "that the distribution of men and women across broad occupational categories added little to the explanation" of the gender wage gap. In other words, wage gaps within occupational categories were as large as those between categories. This may appear to conflict with our remarks above that the inclusion of occupation should explain more of the differential. However, when we remember that only ten categories were used it is not surprising that substantial variation within categories was found. Callan goes on to remark that "investigation using finer occupation classifications would be useful" but adds a cautionary note. Finer and finer classifications would bring us to the point where all the wage gap could be explained, assuming that Gunderson's point on wages within narrowly defined occupations applies in Ireland. But this is not a satisfactory point to arrive at in that it leaves unanswered the question of why men and women occupy different points within the fine occupational categories.

Miller (1987) also addressed the link between occupational segregation and the gender wage gap, but for the UK. He modelled the wage structure taking into account the non-random distribution of individuals across occupations. In essence, his decomposition technique allowed him to derive an estimate of the degree to which both the wage structure and the occupational structure were due to observable differences in the productivity-related characteristics of men and women. In a manner similar to the standard technique, he could then estimate what proportion of the differences in the wage and occupation structures were "unexplained". His results are similar to Callan's (1991). He concludes that "occupational segregation makes only a minor contribution to the gender wage gap". However, he only used six occupational categories in his analysis. As such, it is likely that his strong concluding statement on occupational segregation would be weakened if finer classifications were used. Miller himself makes the point that it cannot be determined "whether analysis with a greater level of occupational detail would affect this result".

Another study on occupational segregation and the wage structure in Ireland is Reilly (1991). He employs a method similar to that of Miller and arrives at a similar result, i.e. that wage differences within occupational categories are more important in explaining the overall wage gap than differences across occupations.[4] Once again though, he is using a small number of occupational categories, in this case five, so it remains a possibility that the wage gaps within occupations are related to men and women holding different jobs and at different levels within occupations.

The common point to emerge from Miller (1987), Callan (1991) and Reilly (1991) is that the use of a highly aggregated classification of occupations in the wage equations used to decompose wage differentials adds little to the explained component. This

---

[4] Reilly (1991) does not provide information on his data set.

could be interpreted as implying that occupational segregation does not help explain the gender wage differential. However, an alternative interpretation is that the occupational classifications used are too broad to capture the difference in more narrowly defined occupations within the broader categories. Whether or not occupational segregation contributes to explaining the gender wage gap is then a definitional matter and depends on how narrowly occupation is defined.

## 4.5 LIMITATIONS OF EXISTING DATA FOR EXAMINING THE LINK BETWEEN OCCUPATIONAL SEGREGATION AND THE GENDER WAGE DIFFERENTIAL

As Callan (1991) noted, analyses using finer occupational classifications would be useful in identifying the nature of the gender wage differential. However, such analyses require very large data sets to ensure that there are sufficient numbers of both men and women in each occupational cell to make reliable statements about the gender wage gap. Most surveys are limited in the degree to which they can be used to address this issue.

Table 2.6 above presented information on female/male wage ratios across a range of occupations. In general, the female-to-male wage ratios within these broadly defined occupations are smaller than the overall figure of 82 per cent. This supports the same conclusion which emerged from Miller (1987), Callan (1991) and Reilly (1991), i.e. that more of the wage gap arises within occupations than between occupations.

In spite of these figures, it would clearly be unwise to conclude from the broad occupational categories that women were being paid less for the same work as men. We would need a much finer series of occupational categories in order to address this. However, the *Living in Ireland Survey* does not contain a sufficient number of individuals for us to be able to cut the data into such fine occupational categories; the numbers in each cell become too small for reliable conclusions to be drawn. The same argument applies if we break the data down by sector. The cell-size difficulties that arise from a finer breakdown by occupation can be seen if we employ the FÁS/ESRI detailed occupational categories. In their series of occupational forecasts, FÁS and the ESRI use 45 occupational categories. If we do the same, we are left with only four categories in which there are at least 25 men and 25 women. As noted in Chapter 2, we avoid calculating ratios when there are fewer than 25 of each sex in a cell because the resulting sample ratios would be highly unreliable estimates of the true ratios in the corresponding population.

Even for those categories with at least 25 men and women, there is a degree of heterogeneity within each to complicate the interpretation of calculated ratios. The four categories are education professionals, clerks, retail sales assistants and other personal service workers. Taking educational professionals as an example, a low wage ratio may emerge because of the distribution of men and women *within* this occupational category: for example, if the higher ranks of university staff are predominantly male, while teachers at primary level are predominantly female.

One immediate response to this might be to simply seek to analyse such issues by looking for detailed wage and salary information from a much larger, but still nationally representative, survey of employees. While this has some advantages in describing the situation, it may not be the most efficient use of resources to address central research questions about the forces giving rise to observed wage gaps, and alternative strategies should also be considered.

The largest regular source of data on labour market issues is the Labour Force Survey, or in more recent years, the Quarterly National Household Survey. This survey has a much larger sample size than the *Living in Ireland Survey*, but does not contain data on wages and salaries. It is possible to use the data to establish how men and women are distributed across occupations and sectors. This has been done in a series of reports by Blackwell (1986, 1989), Durkan (1995) and most recently by Ruane and Sutherland (1999). Combining figures from the three reports, we can present the proportion of women in a range of occupations in 1984, 1993 and 1997.

The degree to which women are more or less concentrated in certain occupations can be seen from Table 4.5. Looking firstly at the figures for 1984 we can see that although 31 per cent of the workforce were women, only 1 per cent of both woodworkers and building and construction workers were women. In contrast, 72 per cent of clerical workers were women. In 1997, when 38 per cent of the workforce were women, the share of women classified as clerical workers had increased to 80 per cent.

*Table 4.5: Proportions of Women in Occupations Listed in 1984, 1993 and 1997*

|  | 1984 | 1993 | 1997 |
|---|---|---|---|
| Occupation | (%) | (%) | (%) |
| Farmers | 4.8 | 6.62 | 6.6 |
| Other agricultural, Forestry and fishery | 22.8 | 12.29 | 14.9 |
| Electrical and electronic | 16.8 | 21.98 | 25.3 |
| Engineering and related trades | 7.0 | 7.26 | 5.3 |
| Woodworkers | 1.0 | 3.19 | 2.9 |
| Leather, leather substitute, textile and clothing | 63.6 | 58.47 | 59.9 |
| Paper and printing | 22.4 | 21.88 | 27.2 |
| Workers in other products | 15.8 | 28.13 | 33.3 |
| Building and construction | 1.0 | 2.56 | 2.8 |
| Foremen and supervisors of manual | 10.1 | 17.36 | 22.5 |
| Labourers and unskilled | 1.4 | 3.79 | 4.6 |
| Transport and communications | 10.9 | 7.74 | 7.6 |
| Warehouse staff, storekeepers, packers and bottlers | 22.4 | 22.01 | 23.8 |
| Clerical workers | 72.2 | 78.23 | 79.9 |
| Proprietors and managers | 20.0 | 26.84 | 28.0 |
| Shop assistants and bar staff | 56.3 | 59.59 | 64.3 |
| Other commercial | 6.4 | 17.94 | 22.0 |
| Professional and technical | 47.5 | 50.89 | 53.1 |
| Service workers | 53.8 | 57.98 | 62.9 |
| Administrative, executive and managerial | 11.0 | 18.95 | 27.4 |
| Others (including not stated) | 7.8 | 9.38 | 19.7 |
| Total | 30.6 | 35.79 | 38.3 |

The share of women among shop assistants and bar staff increased from 56 per cent to 64 per cent over the period 1984 to 1997; over the same period the female share among service workers rose from 54 per cent to 63 per cent. While there are examples of the female share increasing in occupations where they are under-represented, the figures do not reveal any dramatic reduction in occupational segregation. Ruane and Sutherland (1999) note that in 1997, 67 per cent of female employees were in just three occupations.

While this information from the Labour Force Surveys provides an insight into the degree to which occupational segregation exists, the data do not contain information on wages. As such, these data cannot be used to analyse the gender wage differential. One large-scale data set that does contain information on earnings is derived from the Census of Industrial Production. Durkan (1995) and Ruane and Sutherland (1999) present female/male wage ratios for a wide range of industrial sectors. While the data provide much information, they are limited in terms of identifying the sources of the wage gap. It is not possible to say if the wage gaps within each narrow sector are related to human capital characteristics or if they are related to men and women having different occupations within the same sector. In addition, as the information is restricted to industry, it cannot be used to say much about the economy-wide gender wage gap.

## 4.6 RESEARCH PRIORITIES

Over 20 years after the introduction of equal pay legislation, the incidence of unequal pay for the same job is likely to be low. A more likely source of gender pay differences is the difference in the occupations (narrowly defined) that men and women hold. One piece of evidence that supports this claim arises out of the decomposition of the gender wage gap in the public and private sectors. As the pay structure in the public sector is determined by strict administrative rules we can be certain that pay differences across men and women, adjusted for differences in human capital characteristics, are the result of different jobs being held. When we calculate the wage adjustment index, the value will reflect this different distribution of men and women across jobs.

It might be argued that there is more scope for discrimination in the private sector, where legislation may not be reinforced by strict administrative rules. If this were so, then the wage adjustment index would be larger in the private sector than in the public sector. However, when we calculated the indices separately for the public and private sectors it turns out that they are essentially the same. This would suggest that pay differences in the private sector, like the public sector, arise because of the distribution of men and women across jobs and not because of pay differences for men and women doing the same jobs.

Given this hypothesis on the source of the gender wage gap, it would be helpful to have data with sufficiently fine occupational definitions for the hypothesis to be tested. In order to develop a precise picture of the distribution of men and women across narrowly defined occupations, a large-scale sample would be required to ensure observations in each occupation cell.

While such a large-scale sample would provide a snapshot of the distribution of occupations by gender, it would be less useful in establishing the processes whereby men move up the occupational ladder more quickly. Such a process has recently been studied by Booth, Francesconi and Frank (1998). Although much of the discussion of female career progression has emphasised the existence of glass ceiling, Booth et al. have discovered what they describe as a "sticky floor". Drawing on British data, they find no significant differences between the promotion probabilities of men and women. They do, however, find that women enjoy less of a pay advantage following promotion. Their findings contradict the theory proposed by Lazear and Rosen (1990) who viewed women as being less likely to be promoted because of their greater likelihood of spending time out of the labour force. Under the Lazear and Rosen model, women have to be more able than men to achieve promotion. As a result, those women that are promoted are predicted to enjoy higher wages than men in the same grade.

Clearly these alternative views of promotion could be important in the Irish labour market and each could be one of the underlying causes of the gender wage differential. In order to explore such an issue, it is necessary to have data on individuals over time so that the career developments of men and women can be compared. In addition to issues of promotion, the study of career patterns over time would be important in the overall context of understanding the apparent persistent segregation of the Irish workforce. The panel nature of the *Living in Ireland Survey*, with the same individuals being re-interviewed each year since 1994, may make it possible in future to analyse these issues using Irish data. With such data it would be possible to analyse the different career paths of men and women in Ireland in an effort to understand how occupational segregation arises; whether or to what extent it represents a "problem"; and what kinds of policy interventions would be appropriate.

## 4.7 CONCLUSION

Evidence from the 1994 *Living in Ireland Survey* shows that male employees are more likely than female employees to benefit from a variety of non-pay elements of compensation. Pension benefits are the most important of these, in terms of incidence and monetary value. But men are also more likely than women to benefit from free or subsidised health schemes or medical insurance, free or subsidised leisure or sports facilities, and housing-related benefits including subsidised mortgages. A statistical analysis similar to that undertaken with respect to gross wages finds that observed sex differences in the incidence of these non-pay benefits cannot be explained in terms of other characteristics such as age, level of education, or occupation. Thus it seems that non-pay elements add to the observed gap in gross wages between the sexes to make a wider gap in "total compensation". By imputing values for pension benefits and health benefits, we estimated that the female–male wage ratio in 1994 falls from 82.4 per cent to 80.8 per cent.

Theoretical perspectives on discrimination and on gender segregation were reviewed, and the limitations of existing data in examining issues concerning occupational segregation and its impact on the wage differential were outlined. Larger surveys would help to measure the impact of occupational segregation on the wage gap; panel data offers the potential for exploring of the processes underlying occupational segregation.

*Chapter 5*

# International Evidence on Male/Female Wage Differentials

## 5.1 INTRODUCTION

National perceptions of the wage gap between men and women are to some extent shaped by perceptions of where the country stands relative to others. Such perceptions depend in turn on the available international data on this topic. The most widely quoted cross-country statistics on women's earnings relative to men's rely heavily on earnings in manufacturing industry — the sector for which earnings figures tend to be produced most regularly in many countries. For example, the *Human Development Report* (United Nations Development Programme, 1995) and the OECD's *Employment Outlook* (OECD, 1988) both rely heavily on earnings in manufacturing as indicators of male and female earnings across countries.

There are a number of major drawbacks associated with comparisons based on such data. First, as the OECD report makes clear,[1] and as explained in Chapter 2 of the present study, there can be no presumption that the gender wage gap for "production workers in manufacturing" is representative of the gender wage gap in the economy as a whole. Employment in manufacturing is less than one-third of total employment in most advanced economies, and an even smaller proportion of female employment, which tends to be more concentrated in services. The female-to-

---

[1] OECD (1988) uses additional information to provide comparisons based on a broader coverage, but these comparisons are again somewhat limited.

male wage ratio in manufacturing bears no necessary relationship to the economy-wide ratio. Second, the precise coverage of the statistics used tends to vary across countries, rendering them incomparable even for the manufacturing sector. For example, the statistics regularly produced in the UK refer to manual workers in manufacturing; those in Ireland to production workers in manufacturing. Thirdly, the implications of observed differences in male and female wage differentials in any one country, and of differences in gender wage gaps between countries, depend on the extent to which they are explained by productivity-related characteristics.[2] Fourthly, international statistics are often limited in coverage to full-timers (see Waldfogel, 1998).

In this chapter, we begin (Section 5.2) with the most usual cross-country perspective on wage gaps, drawing on regularly produced data for male and female hourly earnings in manufacturing. Section 5.3 then considers some alternative sources of data, and examines an alternative international picture of gross wage gaps for 1994. Finally, we draw on some earlier analysis (Callan et al., 1996) which examines how the interpretation of this cross-country evidence on gross wage gaps might be altered if "unexplained" wage gaps could be estimated across countries with an approach similar to that adopted in Chapter 3.

## 5.2 INTERNATIONAL TRENDS IN THE FEMALE-TO-MALE WAGE RATIO

Neither levels nor trends in the female-to-male wage ratio for manufacturing industry can be taken as representative of economy-wide developments. Nevertheless, international comparisons based on the wage gaps in manufacturing industry are commonly made, for lack of other suitable data. When countries are ranked by the female-to-male wage ratio, the Scandinavian countries usually emerge at the top of the "league tables", with ratios of between 80 to 90 per cent in recent years. Figure 5.1

---

[2] A further difficulty is that the elements of self-selection in the processes by which individuals choose to participate in the labour market, and become employed, may result in a male–female gap in potential or "offered" wages which differs from the "observed" wage gap. We return to this issue in the Irish context in Chapter 7.

shows the evolution of the female-to-male wage ratio in manufacturing industry for Ireland[3] and for the Scandinavian countries. It can be seen that the wage ratio started out lower in Ireland than in Scandinavia, and that by the late 1980s a gap of
between 8 and 22 percentage points remained between Ireland
and Sweden. More recent data suggests that the wage gap has
fallen in Ireland, but has also fallen in Norway (the only Scandinavian country for which data are available from the ILO's *Bulletin of Labour Statistics*), leaving the Irish ratio some 13 percentage
points below Norway's.

**Figure 5.1: Female-to-Male Wage Ratios, Ireland and Scandinavia**

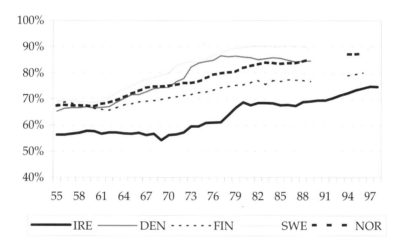

Figure 5.2 shows the evolution of the Irish wage ratio relative to
the UK, the US, Australia and Japan. The Irish wage ratio has
tended to remain quite close to that of the UK, as might be expected given the close links between the two labour markets.[4] The
stability in the female-to-male wage ratio in the US has been the
subject of considerable study: some of the factors underpinning
this stability include increased participation by women with low-

---

[3] The steep rise in the wage ratio in Ireland during the 1970s coincides with the
introduction of equality legislation in 1974 and 1977 (see Chapters 1 and 8).

[4] Equality legislation was introduced in the UK in 1970 and 1975.

wage characteristics, and a rise in inequality of earnings — a factor explored in the Irish context in the next chapter.

*Figure 5.2: Female-to-Male Wage Ratios, Ireland, UK, US, Japan and Australia*

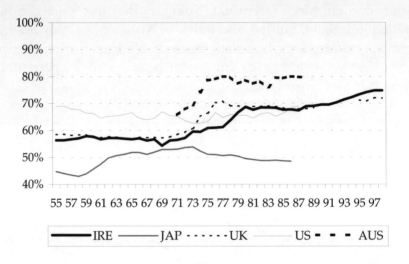

*Figure 5.3: Female-to-Male Wage Ratios, Ireland, Germany, Holland and France*

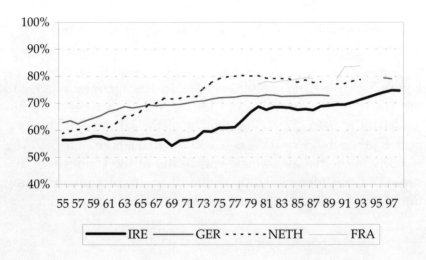

A comparison with Continental European countries shows a persistent gap between the Irish wage ratio and that of France and the Netherlands, though with some convergence towards the German ratio.

The evolution of these wage ratios over time is subject to influences from policy changes (such as equal pay and anti-discrimination legislation, and minimum wages) but is also substantially influenced by the balance of supply and demand for male and female labour. The markets for male and female labour cannot be regarded as either perfectly integrated nor completely segregated. In most OECD countries, despite rapid expansion in female labour force participation, the occupational and industrial structure of female employment remains different from that of men. Thus, if industries in which women are concentrated experience relatively strong growth, women's earnings may be bid up relative to men's; but if the supply of female labour increases, tending to depress wage growth in such sectors, downward pressure on the female-to-male wage ratio may result.

## 5.3 BROADER INTERNATIONAL COMPARISONS

We have pointed out the limitations of international comparisons of female-to-male wage ratios calculated for manufacturing industry. But are more representative data available? A search of internationally comparable data sources reveals two potential sources[5] with a wider coverage than simply manufacturing industry:

1.  Structure of Earnings Statistics (SES), gathered in every member state of the EU, typically for the year 1995.

2.  The European Community Household Panel (ECHP), which began in 1994.

A recent Eurostat publication based on the Structure of Earnings Statistics data (Benassi, 1999) compares male–female wage differentials across all EU countries except Ireland (due to confidentiality restrictions on the use of the data). However, it must be noted

---

[5] Each of these sources is co-ordinated by Eurostat.

that the data in the survey are restricted to firms employing 10 or more workers, and also exclude employees in public administration, health and social work, other community, social and personal service activities. As Benassi (1999) states, "the coverage of the survey is not ideal to study women's earnings because sectors where there are a majority of women are not covered: health, education and personal services".

The ECHP, of which the *Living in Ireland Survey* is a part, is a household survey, which in principle includes employees from all sectors. We have undertaken a special analysis of the first wave (1994) results across Europe (with the exception of Germany, because of restrictions on the availability of the data) which are presented in Table 5.1.

*Table 5.1: Female to Male Wage Ratios for All Employees, ECHP, 1994*

|                | Female Wage as % of Male Wage |
|----------------|:---------------------------:|
| United Kingdom | 73.9                        |
| Ireland        | 80.8                        |
| France         | 83.9                        |
| Luxembourg     | 84.9                        |
| Spain          | 85.9                        |
| Belgium        | 87.8                        |
| Greece         | 88.4                        |
| Denmark        | 89.1                        |
| Portugal       | 92.2                        |
| Italy          | 94.3                        |

These data suggest that the wage gap is highest in the UK, where the average female wage is about three-quarters of the average male wage. The next largest gap is in Ireland, where the average female wage (estimated on the ECHP dataset for Ireland, which differs somewhat from the main national dataset used in this study) is about 81 per cent of the male wage. In other EU countries, women's wages average between 84 per cent and 94 per cent of the male wage.

While these data are more comprehensive than those typically used in international comparisons, they are still measuring the "observed" labour market gap in wages. They do not take into account the differences in labour market characteristics of women and men across countries. It is to this topic that we now turn.

## 5.4 WAGE GAPS ADJUSTED FOR PRODUCTIVITY-RELATED CHARACTERISTICS

Callan et al. (1995) assembled cross-country survey data for six countries — including some from the top, bottom and middle of the usual international league tables, based on male–female wage gaps in manufacturing — and compared the rankings based on female to male wage ratios in manufacturing, economy-wide survey data, and survey-based estimates with adjustments using wage equations. Callan et al. make it clear that the ratios of hourly wages studied in that paper are not a complete index of economic opportunities facing women, or of the economic position of women relative to men. The general perception of the Scandinavian countries as leading the world in terms of gender equity is based on more than simply female-to-male wage ratios: a battery of other policies (such as widely available and heavily subsidised childcare facilities, and parental leave arrangements) facilitate fuller participation by women in economic life in these countries. But on the specific issue of the relative hourly pay of men and women, the statistics derived by Callan et al. from comparable sources suggest some interesting conclusions. The findings are summarised in Table 5.2.

The extent of the gaps between countries included in the analysis seems to be somewhat overstated by the figures based on workers in manufacturing: figures based on harmonised analyses of household surveys find some degree of convergence around a higher central tendency. There are also some changes in intercountry rankings, suggesting that the hourly earnings in manufacturing should not be relied upon as an accurate indicator even of the rankings of countries in terms of gender wage gaps. Furthermore, a simple human capital specification, based on educational qualifications and years worked, suggests that wage ratios adjusted for these variables converge still more, around a higher mean. One potential implication is that policies facilitating high female participation may help to raise the female-to-male wage ratios in other countries closer to the Swedish level.[6]

*Table 5.2: Female/Male Wage Ratios: Manufacturing Vs All Employments, Selected Countries*

| | Year | Workers in Mfg (ILO)[1] | All Workers in All Industries (Surveys)[1] | |
|---|---|---|---|---|
| | | | *Unadjusted Ratio* | *Adjusted using Wage Equation Including Years Worked* |
| Sweden | 1986 | 90.1 *(1)* | 92.2 *(1)* | 89.1 *(1)* |
| East Germany | 1991 | 86.1 *(2)* | 79.1 *(4)* | 83.6 *(4)* |
| Denmark | 1990 | 84.6 *(3)* | 77.2 *(5)* | 84.2 *(3)* |
| Australia | 1989 | 80.4 *(4)* | 89.9 *(2)* | n.a. |
| West Germany | 1991 | 73.2 *(5)* | 75.0 *(6)* | 81.9 *(5)* |
| United Kingdom | 1991 | 67.9 *(6)* | 70.8 *(7)* | 76.6 *(6)* |
| Ireland | 1987 | 67.4 *(7)* | 80.1 *(3)* | 85.3 *(2)* |
| Mean[2] | | 78.5 | 80.6 | 83.5 |
| Coefficient of variation[2] | | 10.7 | 8.9 | 4.5 |

*Notes:*  1. Country rankings are italicised, in parentheses.
         2. Mean and coefficient of variation (standard deviation divided by mean) are unweighted.

*Source:*  Callan et al. (1995).

## 5.5 CONCLUSIONS

There are greater difficulties in making international comparisons of male–female wage differentials than are commonly realised. General perceptions are shaped by the most regularly produced and readily available data, which are for men and women in manufacturing industry. But even the international rankings based on this cannot be taken as indicative of international rank-

---

[6] Lower levels of inequality of wage rates ("wage compression") in the Scandinavian countries may also contribute to higher female-to-male wage ratios in those countries, for reasons to be discussed in Chapter 6.

ings on an economy-wide basis. Data released recently from the European Community Household Panel, and analysed here, suggest that the wage gap is greatest in the UK. The wage gap in Ireland in 1994 was estimated as smaller than in the UK, but greater than in other European countries. This may reflect lower participation rates in paid employment of women in Ireland, relative to their European counterparts, because once adjusted for experience the Irish gap is relatively small.

*Chapter 6*

# Earnings Inequality and the Distribution of Gender Wage Differences, 1987–1994

## 6.1 INTRODUCTION

The traditional approach to examining gender-based wage differences has focused on decomposing the average wage gap into the portion which can be explained by differences in characteristics and the unexplained portion which is attributed to discrimination.[1] However, focusing on average wage differences provides only a partial explanation of the gender wage gap. In this chapter we argue that a more comprehensive analysis of gender wage differences can be obtained by taking the entire distribution of wages into account.

There are two important reasons for looking at the entire distribution. Firstly an average wage differential of, say, 10 per cent is consistent not only with a situation in which all women are underpaid by 10 per cent but also with one in which half of the women are underpaid by 20 per cent and the other half receive the same wages as men. Although the average wage gap is equal in both these cases, one's view of the relative importance of wage discrimination and of the appropriate policy to combat discrimination may depend on the distribution of the wage gains. A given policy instrument may reduce discrimination significantly for a sizeable proportion of the population (Group A) yet it may have little effect on a minority of women (Group B) whose wages re-

---

[1] For examples of this approach see Oaxaca (1973), Neumark (1988), Callan and Wren (1994) and Chapter 3 of this study.

main very low relative to male wages. Would this policy be preferred to one whose impact on the wage gap is smaller for Group
A but whose effect is distributed more evenly (i.e. the effect is
larger for Group B)? The answer to this question depends on the
costs of both measures but also on how policy makers aggregate
over the distribution of wage gains (the simple average wage gap
assigns equal weights to all wage difference regardless of size).
Clearly, knowledge of the distribution of wage differences is essential if one is to distinguish between these policies.

The second reason for focusing on the entire distribution of
wages is to distinguish between the impact of gender-specific
forces on relative wages and more general changes in the wage
structure which, other things being equal, affect all workers regardless of gender. To see how this may be important consider the
growth in wage inequality which has occurred in many developed countries over the last decade.[2,3] While this change in the
wage structure is skill biased, and not gender biased, it may still
have an important effect on the wage gap between men and
women. To the extent that female workers are located in the lower
part of the wage distribution, any changes that reduce/increase
inequality will favour/hurt female workers disproportionately
and thus lead to a fall/rise in the male–female wage gap. Simply
observing a rise in the male–female wage gap at a time when
inequality is increasing cannot be taken as evidence of increased
discrimination even in the absence of any changes in underlying
productivity differences. Distinguishing between gender-specific
forces and more general changes in the wage structure requires a
full distributional analysis.

The next section of this chapter discusses the data used in our
analysis and describes the distribution of wages for males and
females in 1987 and 1994. In discussing the distribution of wages
we also outline the implications of these distributions for the proposed introduction of the national minimum wage. Section 6.3

---

[2] For a discussion of these changes in an international context see Gottschalk and
Smeeding (1997).

[3] For an overview of the possible explanations for this increase see the articles
contained in the *Journal of Economic Perspectives*, Vol. 11, No. 2.

summarises the distribution of "wage adjustment indices"[4] throughout the female population. Section 6.4 provides a more detailed analysis of the movements in the female–male wage ratio over time, paying particular attention to the impact of general changes in the wage structure of the male–female wage gap.

## 6.2 MALE AND FEMALE WAGE DISTRIBUTIONS AND THE PROPOSED NATIONAL MINIMUM WAGE

The analysis in this paper uses data from the ESRI *Living in Ireland* surveys conducted in 1987 and 1994. We restrict our attention to employees for whom an hourly wage could be constructed from the data on gross wages and hours worked who have valid wage data. Thus, for 1987, there were 1,215 male employees and 778 female employees, while for 1994 there were 1,917 men and 1,390 women. Table 6.1 provides summary statistics on the distribution of male and female hourly wages in both years. These statistics are produced on an unweighted basis, so as to facilitate later analysis; they are not, therefore, comparable with the weighted statistics designed to represent national trends used in Chapter 2.

The results in this table highlight two important features of the wage structure in Ireland, which will form the basis of the analysis in our chapter. From the second-last row of the table we can see that in 1987 average female wages were approximately 77 per cent of average males wages. By 1994 this had risen to 84 per cent. In this chapter we will examine the extent to which the difference in male and female wages at a point in time reflect differences in characteristics or other forces such as discrimination. In particular we present evidence on the distribution of the latter component throughout the population. Furthermore we will seek to examine the forces behind the increase in the female–male wage ratio over time. As mentioned in the introduction, it is important that we control for general changes in the wage structure when examining changes in the male–female wage gap over time. Evidence that such changes may be important are given in the last row of Table 6.1 which shows that for men, in particular, wage inequality has

---

[4] More commonly termed "discrimination indices" in the economics literature, but for reasons set out in Chapter 3, we use the term "wage adjustment index" here.

increased over this period.[5] Given that female workers are located in the lower end of the wage distribution, any changes that increase inequality will tend to reduce the female–male wage ratio. This needs to be taken into account in examining changes in the gender pay gap over time.

*Table 6.1 Summary Statistics on the Distribution of Male and Female Wages*

|  | 1987 | | 1994 | |
|---|---|---|---|---|
|  | *Male* | *Female* | *Male* | *Female* |
| Median | £4.66 | £3.56 | £6.15 | £5.00 |
| *Others as % of median* | | | | |
| 10th percentile | 54 | 48 | 46 | 50 |
| 25% | 77 | 71 | 71 | 70 |
| 75% | 138 | 142 | 148 | 153 |
| 90% | 203 | 215 | 220 | 240 |
| Mean | £5.50 | £4.26 | £7.42 | £6.22 |
| Female-to-male wage ratio | 77% | | 84% | |
| Coefficient of variation | 0.61 | 0.65 | 0.66 | 0.66 |

Figures 6.1 and Figure 6.2 (see page 90) plot the distribution of both male and female wages in 1987 and 1994 respectively. Both the higher level of mean wages and the greater variability in male wages are evident from this graph. These graphs also help us understand the likely consequences of the introduction of a minimum wage on the gender wage gap. We consider three alternative levels for a minimum wage £3.00, £3.25 and £3.50 in 1994 prices. The £3.25 figure cuts off about the same proportion of the wage distribution as the figure of £4.40 envisaged for the year 2000 in the government's minimum wage proposals.

Table 6.2 examines the likely effect of the minimum wage on the gender wage gap by estimating the new gender gap if all

---

[5] For a more general discussion of wage inequality in Ireland see Nolan and Hughes (1998).

workers currently being paid below the cut-off points were moved up to the cut-off points.[6] The results show that the introduction of a minimum wage will have a relatively small impact on the gender gap — perhaps less than 1 percentage point. On average male workers would still earn over 17 per cent more than female workers even at the highest level of the minimum wage examined (£3.50 in 1994 prices). The results clearly show that the impact of a minimum wage on the gender gap varies with the level of the minimum wage. A minimum wage set at £3 an hour would have very little impact on the gender gap. This is not surprising when one looks at the densities presented in Figure 6.3 (page 91). We see that there is very little difference in the proportion of men and women with very low pay (£2 an hour or less), as a result of which minimum wages in this region can have little impact on the gender pay gap.

*Table 6.2: Impact of a Minimum Wage on the Female-to-Male Wage Ratio*

| Minimum Wage Level (1994 terms) | Average Male Wage | Average Female Wage | Female to Male Wage Ratio (%) |
|---|---|---|---|
| None | 7.42 | 6.22 | 83.8 |
| £3 | 7.52 | 6.34 | 84.1 |
| £3.25 | 7.56 | 6.39 | 84.5 |
| £3.50 | 7.60 | 6.48 | 85.3 |

[a] The £3.25 figure cuts off about the same proportion of the wage distribution as the figure of £4.40 envisaged for the year 2000 in the government's minimum wage proposals.

---

[6] This analysis is static in that it assumes that workers currently paid below the minimum wage retain their jobs. For a discussion of the debate relating to job losses arising from a minimum wage see Card and Krueger (1995) or Dickens et al. (1993) who argue that the job losses tend to be very small, or Murphy and Walsh (1996) or Neumark and Wascher (1998) whose research suggest larger job losses.

## 6.3 DISTRIBUTION OF THE DISCRIMINATION INDEX

The traditional approach to measuring discrimination is described in Chapter 3. The approach focuses on decomposing the gap in average wages into a part that relates to differences in the *average* characteristics of men and women and a part that cannot be explained by such differences in characteristics — a residual that may be due to discrimination. Jenkins (1994) proposes a new approach to measuring discrimination. The key element of this approach is predicting how much *each* female would receive if her characteristics were valued as male characteristics. We call this the female reference wage and denote it as $r_i$ and estimate it using regression techniques described in Appendix 6.1.[7] This is compared to the wages women actually receive in the market (called $y_i$.) The measure $(r_i - y_i)/y_i$, which we denote by $S_i$ tells us the percentage increase in female wages if characteristics are held constant but valued according to the male wage structure. For women experiencing discrimination we would expect $S_i$ to be positive; that is, these woman would be paid more if her characteristics were rewarded as males.

From this analysis we obtain a distribution of potential wage changes (one for each female). An important question is how to present this information. The traditional approach is simply to report the average values of these wage gaps. However, as mentioned earlier this approach may hide significant differences at both ends of the distribution (i.e., women who fare better when treated like men and women who may actually be worse off if paid like men). An alternative is to look at the entire distribution.

Summary statistics for this distribution are given in Table 6.3 and the entire distribution of S is presented in Figures 6.4 and 6.5 (pages 91–92). Looking at Table 6.3, we see that although the average level of the "discrimination index" or "wage adjustment index" has fallen substantially between 1987 and 1994 (a result consistent with that reported in Chapter 3), focusing on the average does indeed hide significant variation in wage discrimination throughout the distribution. For instance in 1994 average female wages would have been expected to rise by approximately 5 per

---

[7] The regression results used to calculate $r_i$ are given in Table A.6.1.

cent if their characteristics were rewarded according to the male wage structure. However, one can see from Table 6.3 that, for 10 per cent of the female population, the estimated increase would have been in the order of 25 per cent. Furthermore we see that a significant minority of women (approximately 25 per cent in 1994) would *be worse off* if paid according to the male reward structure. This is quite different from results found in the UK studies using this approach (e.g. Jenkins, 1994; Makepeace *et al.*, 1999). Our analysis suggests that these women are likely to be more educated, older workers and work predominantly in the professional occupations. These results make it clear that a simple "one for all" policy towards gender wage discrimination is unlikely to be the most efficient way of tackling the problem. The extent to which female wages would increase if paid according to the male structure varies substantially and this needs to be taken into account when addressing the gender wage gap.

*Table 6.3: Distribution of "Discrimination Index"*

| | 1987 | 1994 |
|---|---|---|
| D | 17.5 | 5.60 |
| Percentiles $(r_i - y_i)/y_i$ | | |
| 1 % | −0.13 | −0.21 |
| 5% | −0.09 | −0.15 |
| 10% | −0.04 | −0.12 |
| 25% | 0.13 | −0.05 |
| 50% | 0.18 | 0.04 |
| 75% | 0.22 | 0.14 |
| 90% | 0.26 | 0.24 |
| 95% | 0.34 | 0.31 |
| 99% | 0.50 | 0.58 |
| Mean | 0.16 | 0.055 |

## 6.4 WAGE STRUCTURE AND GENDER DIFFERENTIALS

While the previous section of this chapter looked at the distribution of discrimination, the procedure used there is unable to dis-

tinguish between what we might call "gender-neutral" changes in
the wage structure and "gender-specific" changes in wages. Recent work by Callan (1997) has shown that there has been a significant increase in wage inequality in Ireland over the last ten
years (in fact the increase in wage inequality in Ireland between
1987 and 1994 was as large as that experienced in any of the other
countries studied). Since female workers are located in the lower
part of the wage distribution, any changes that increase inequality
will hurt female workers disproportionately and thus lead to a
rise in the male–female wage gap. Alternatively, if incomes policies were reducing wage dispersion we might expect to see a fall
in the male–female wage gap. We call these effects gender-neutral
effects in that they reflect changes in the general wage structure
and are not as a result of something specific to females. Given the
increase in inequality that has occurred over this period, it is important that we control for gender-neutral changes before we can
accurately assess the importance of reductions in discrimination.
One could imagine a situation where reductions in discrimination
have improved the relative position of females substantially.
However, if at the same time changes in the wage structure are
making the market less favourable for all low wage workers (of
which women form the majority) then one might observe very
little change in the female–male wage gap. Blau and Kahn (1991)
liken such a situation to attempts to "swim against the tide". Significant effort may be exerted to improve one's position but other
forces are at work to counteract these efforts. Indeed, they argue
that the substantial wage inequality observed in the United States
can explain why the gender wage gap in the US has tended to be
larger than in many developed countries despite the fact that female workers in the US have relatively high qualifications and
that the United States has seemingly had a longer and stronger
commitment to anti-discrimination legislation laws than most
economically advanced nations.

Given the fact that wage inequality in Ireland is among the
highest in the OECD and that the increase in wage inequality observed in Ireland in recent times has been larger than that observed in other countries it is important that we identify the
impact of inequality on the gender gap. The results of this analysis
may be important in that they may direct us to institutional fea-

tures of the wage-setting process that may be important determinants of the gender pay gap in Ireland.

To examine the likely impact of changes in inequality on the gender gap, we examine the relative position of females in the male wage distribution. In 1987 the wages of the median woman corresponded to the 24th percentile of the male distribution but by 1994 the wages of the median woman had increased to the 34th percentile of the male distribution. Clearly women have been improving their position over time. However, while this has been taking place there have been also forces working against low skill workers in general (as reflected in growing wage inequality) which may disproportionately affect women.

To see this formally, consider the wage decompositions presented in Chapter 3.

$$\Delta \overline{W}^{87} = \overline{W}_m^{87} - \overline{W}_f^{87} = \Delta \overline{X}^{87} \beta_m^{87} - \overline{X}_f^{87} \Delta \beta^{87} + (\alpha_m^{87} \overline{H}_m^{87} - \alpha_f^{87} \overline{H}_f^{87})$$

$$= \Delta \overline{X}^{87} \beta_m^{87} - \overline{U}_f^{87} + \Delta Z^{87}$$

where

$$\Delta \overline{X}^{87} = (\overline{X}_m^{87} - \overline{X}_f^{87}); \quad \Delta \beta^{87} = (\beta_f^{87} - \beta_m^{87}); \quad \Delta Z^{87} = (\alpha_m^{87} \overline{H}_m^{87} - \alpha_f^{87} \overline{H}_f^{87})$$

and $\quad \overline{U}_f^{87} = \overline{X}_f^{87} \Delta \beta^{87}$

Taking the difference in the average wage differential between 1994 and 1987, we get:

$$\Delta \overline{W}^{94} - \Delta \overline{W}^{87} = (\Delta \overline{X}^{94} - \Delta \overline{X}^{87}) \beta_m^{87} + \Delta \overline{X}^{94} (\beta_m^{94} - \beta_m^{87}) - (\overline{U}_f^{94} - \overline{U}_f^{87}) + (\Delta Z^{94} - \Delta Z^{87})$$

The first term in the above expression measures changes in the wage gap resulting from changes in the observed productivity gap evaluated at the male market price. The second term reflects the impact of observable changes in the wage structure on the average wage gap. In keeping with Juhn et al. (1991) and Blau and Kahn (1992, 1994), we call this the "observable price effect". However, it is important to understand that this term measures the impact of changes in returns to characteristics over time and not differences between male and female rates of return. The third term in brackets captures changes in the residual component over time and is generally thought of as measuring changes in discrimination, while the final term captures the impact of spells not working.

*Table 6.4: Decomposition of the Wage Gap over Time*

|  |  | 1987–1994 |
|---|---|---|
| Change in Log Wage Differential |  | −.118 |
| Observables | Quantity $(\Delta X^{94}-\Delta X^{87})\beta_m^{87}$ | −.071 |
|  | Prices $\Delta X^{94} (\beta_m^{94}-\beta_m^{87})$ | .05 |
| Years not worked | $(\Delta Z^{94}-\Delta Z^{87})$ | .002 |
| Unobservables | Residual $-(U_f^{94}-U_f^{87})$ | −.0987 |

The results for this decomposition are presented in Table 6.4. The first row shows the actual change in the log wage gap over time and rows 2–5 show the contribution of observable skills, observable prices (both omitting the influence of years not worked), years not worked and the residual term to this change. The log wage gap between men and women fell by .118 between 1987 and 1994. The decomposition results indicate that the important factors driving this fall were a reduction in observable skill differences and a fall in the residual component. The impact of observable prices on the wage differential is given in the third row. The result is as expected given the earlier discussion concerning the rise in wage inequality. An important component of this increase in wage inequality has been an increase in the returns to skills such as education and work experience. As the returns to these skills increase, workers who possess relatively few of these skills fall behind those more skilled. This trend results not only in an increase in wage inequality (as documented in Barrett et al., 1999) but also in a rise in the male–female wage gap, for the simple reason that women tend to be less skilled than men. Indeed, our results show that the increase in the returns to skill between 1987 and 1994 would have resulted in the log wage gap increasing by .05. Changes in factors associated with years out of work appear to have little impact on changes in the male–female wage differential between 1987 and 1994.

The above result highlights the importance of the residual term in explaining the improvements in relative female wages in Ireland between 1987 and 1994. However, work by Juhn et al. (1991) showed that the residual component can itself be decomposed into a "quantity" and a "price" effect.[8] For the residual component, the quantity effect captures changes in unmeasured characteristics of women relative to men, as well as changes in discrimination practices. Following Blau and Kahn (1991), we call this the "gap effect". The residual price effect, on the other hand, measures changes in the returns to the unmeasured characteristics. In keeping with the literature, we label changes in observed characteristics and the gap effect as "gender specific" effects, and changes in the wage differential arising from prices (both observed and unobserved) as "wage structure" effects.

The results of this extended decomposition are given in Table 6.5. The top panel summarises the performance of females relative to males over this period. The first row shows the raw male–female wage gap, which was approximately 30 per cent in 1987 but had fallen to 17 per cent in 1994. The second row contains the residual effects presented in earlier estimation. As mentioned earlier, these figures provide estimates of the male–female wage gap once differences in observable characteristics are taken into account. The third column shows the comparable male worker for the median female in the residual distribution. Two features emerge from this row. We see that females tend to be located in the tail of the residual distribution (the median female in 1987 corresponded to only the 32nd percentile male in this year). As a result of this, any increase in the return to unobserved characteristics will tend to hurt female workers disproportionately (the unobservable price effect). We also note that women have being moving up the residual distribution over time as a result of improvements in unobserved characteristics or reductions in discrimination (the gap effect).

The results of the decomposition are given in the lower panel of the table. The observed effects are as reported in Table 6.4,

---

[8] The technical details of this decomposition are given in Appendix 6.2.

while the unobserved effects decompose the residual component into the "gap effect" and the "unobserved price effect". Looking at the unobserved effect we see that almost all of the residual effect reported in Table 6.4 reflects changes in the gap effect; that is, improvements in unobserved female characteristics or reduced discrimination. Movements in unobserved prices seem to have only had a small negative effect on female wages. This is in contrast to the relatively large effect from the return to measured prices.

*Table 6.5 Decomposition of Changes in the Wage Gap Over Time*

| | | 1987 | 1994 |
|---|---|---|---|
| Log Wage Differential | | .289 | .171 |
| Mean Female Residual | | −.143 | −.044 |
| Mean Female Percentile in Male Residual distribution | | 31.7 | 42.1 |
| Decomposition of Change in Differential | | | 87–94 |
| Change in log wage differential 1994–1987 | | | −.118 |
| Observables | Observed X's $(\Delta X^{94} - \Delta X^{87})\beta_m^{87}$ | | −.071 |
| | Observed Prices $\Delta X^{94}(\beta_m^{94} - \beta_m^{87})$ | | +.050 |
| | $(\Delta Z^{94} - \Delta Z^{87})$ | | .002 |
| Unobservables | Gap | | −.105 |
| | Unobservable prices | | +.006 |
| Gender Specific | | | −.176 |
| Wage Structure | | | .056 |
| Z term | | | .002 |

The last three rows summarise the overall contribution of gender specific effects, wage structure effects and years not worked to the fall in the male–female wage gap between 1987 and 1994. Changes in years not worked have had very little impact on the change in the wage differential over this period. The other two components show that while Irish women have being making significant improvements relative to men over this period (gender specific effects), they have being doing so in a market which has become more unfavourable for low wage workers (wage structure effect). The significant increase in wage inequality in Ireland over this period has increased the penalty associated with being low skilled.

While women have being improving their skills over time, they still tend to be located in the lower end of the skill distribution.[9] These two facts combined have acted as a brake on the increase in the female-to-male wage ratio in Ireland.

## 6.5 CONCLUSION

This chapter takes a distributional approach to analysing male–female wage differences in Ireland. In the first part of the chapter, we examine the likely effects of the proposed national minimum wage on the male–female wage gap. Our estimates of the first round effects indicate that a minimum wage of £3.25 an hour in 1994 (roughly corresponding to the £4.40 envisaged for the year 2000) would increase the female-to-male wage ratio by just under 1 percentage point. The estimated impact varies in a non-linear fashion as the level of the minimum wage is changed. We then extended the traditional approach to estimating discrimination by examining not just the average wages of men and women but rather the entire distribution of such wages. In particular, we compare the wages actually received by women to what they would have received if paid like men. On average, we find that in 1994 female wages would have been expected to rise by approximately 5 per cent if their characteristics were rewarded according to the male pay structure. However, there is substantial variation around this average. In fact, we find that almost 25 per cent of women would be worse off if paid according to the male reward structure. These workers tend to be older, more educated, and work predominantly in the professional sector. On the other hand more than 10 per cent of females would see their wages improve

---

[9] The term "skill" here, as elsewhere in the chapter, includes characteristics such as length of labour market experience.

by almost 25 per cent if paid according to the male pay structure. Policies aimed at achieving wage parity should take these differences into account.

The final section of the chapter examines changes in the wage gap between 1987 and 1994 taking into account the fact that changes in wage inequality which have occurred in Ireland over this period. In particular, we argued that more egalitarian pay structures are likely to be associated with lower gender pay gaps. This is important in an Irish setting when we realise that wage inequality in Ireland is high relative to OECD levels and furthermore the recent increases in wage inequality in Ireland have tended to exceed those observed in other developed countries. Our results confirm the detrimental impact that increased wage inequality has had on the gender wage gap in Ireland. Had the level of wage inequality remained unchanged between 1987 and 1994, the log wage gap would have fallen by .18 (due to improvements in skill levels and reductions in the "unexplained gap" between men's and women's wages). However, the increase in wage inequality over the period resulted in the log wage differential only falling by .11.

## APPENDIX 6.1 REGRESSION RESULTS

### *Table A.6.1: Regression Results*

|  | 1987 | | 1994 | |
|---|---|---|---|---|
|  | *Women* | *Men* | *Women* | *Men* |
| Constant | .43 (.078) | .69 (.055) | 1.079 (.063) | .660 (.048) |
| Junior/Inter Cert | .11 (.051) | .12 (.032) | .086 (.042) | .210 (.032) |
| Leaving Cert | .37 (.051) | .33 (.035) | .259 (.041) | .381 (.034) |
| Diploma | .68 (.068) | .48 (.051) | .430 (.053) | .560 (.046) |
| University | 1.03 (.072) | .74 (.048) | .916 (.051) | .993 (.040) |
| Years in paid work | .07 (.0049) | .06 (.0031) | .062 (.004) | .068 (.003) |
| (Years paid work)$^2$ | −.001 (.0013) | −.0001 (.00006) | −.0011 (.0001) | −.001 (.0001) |
| Urban | .07 (.043) | .07 (.030) | .054 (.026) | .113 (.024) |
| Dublin | .06 (.045) | .003 (.032) | .051 (.028) | .060 (.026) |
| Completed apprenticeship | −.13 (.071) | .001 (.027) | −.031 (.081) | .043 (.030) |
| Unemployment rate in occupation | −.66 (.507) | −.88 (.21) | −.683 (.24) | −.026 (.142) |
| Unemployment rate in industry | .52 (.25) | .55 (.13) | −2.14 (.245) | −.026 (.170) |
| Years not in paid work | −.02 (.0068) | −.03 (.0080) | −.014 (.004) | −.016 (.007) |
| (Years not in paid work)$^2$ | .001 (.00028) | .001 (.00026) | .0004 (.0001) | .0012 (.0003) |
| N | 778 | 1215 | 1390 | 1917 |

*Figure 6.1: Distribution of Male Wages, 1987 and 1994*

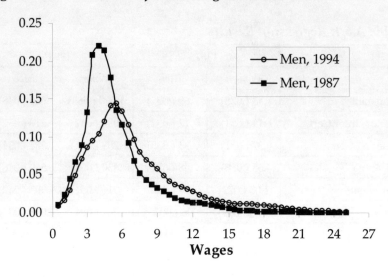

*Figure 6.2: Distribution of Female Wages, 1987 and 1994*

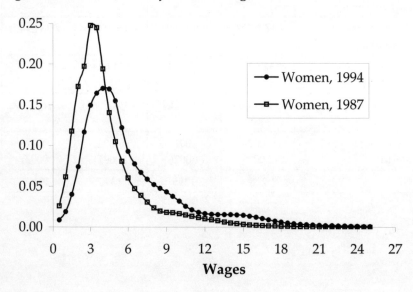

*Figure 6.3: Distribution of Male and Female Wage, 1994*

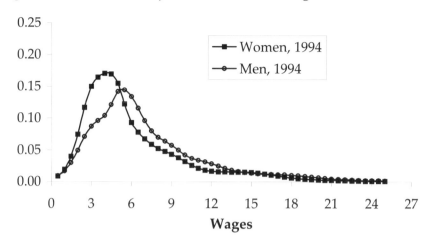

*Figure 6.4: Distribution of "Wage Adjustment Index" in 1987*

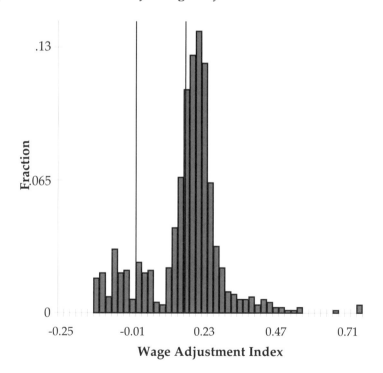

*Figure 6.5: Distribution of "Wage Adjustment Index" in 1994*

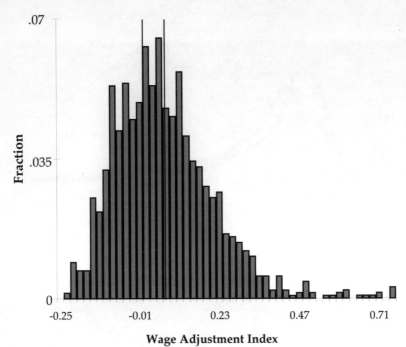

**Wage Adjustment Index**

## APPENDIX 6.2 TECHNICAL DETAILS OF JENKINS MEASURE OF DISCRIMINATION

Consider the following two wage regressions:

$$W_m^o = X_m^o \beta_m^o + V_m^o \tag{6.1}$$

$$W_f^o = X_f^o \beta_f^o + V_f^o \tag{6.2}$$

We use the estimates from these regressions to construct the reference wage ($r_i$) and the actual wage $y_i$ as:

$$r_i = \exp(Xb_m) \; i \in \text{Women} \tag{6.3}$$

$$y_i = \exp(Xb_w) \; i \in \text{Women} \tag{6.4}$$

That is, $r_i$ measures the wage a woman could expect to earn if paid according to the male wage structure, while $y_i$ measures the expected female wage predicted using the female wage structure.

The traditional measure of discrimination is:

$$D = 100[\exp(\overline{S}) - 1] \text{ where } \overline{S} \approx \text{mean}[(r_i - y_i)/y_i] \text{ } i \in \text{Women} \quad (6.5)$$

## APPENDIX 6.3 TECHNICAL DESCRIPTION OF THE JUHN-MURPHY-PIERCE DECOMPOSITION

As shown in the text, the difference in the average wage differential between 1987 and 1994 is given as:

$$\overline{\Delta W^{94}} - \overline{\Delta W^{87}} = (\overline{\Delta X^{94}} - \overline{\Delta X^{87}})\beta_m^{87} + \overline{\Delta X^{94}}(\beta_m^{94} - \beta_m^{87}) + (\Delta Z^{94} - \Delta Z^{87}) - (\overline{U_f^{94}} - \overline{U_f^{87}})$$

$$(6.6)$$

The first term measures changes in the wage gap resulting from changes in the observed productivity gap evaluated at the male market price. The second term reflects the impact of observable changes in the wage structure on the average wage gap. The third term in brackets accounts for the effect of changes in time out of employment. The fourth term captures changes in the residual component over time and is generally thought of as measuring changes in discrimination.

The residual is normally associated with discrimination. However, we can also think of it as consisting of a gender-specific component and a wage-structure component. To see this, we follow JMP and rewrite our basic wage equation for male workers in year 0 as:

$$W_m^o = X_m^o \beta_m^o + \sigma_m^o \theta_m^o \quad (6.7)$$

where

$$\theta_m^o = \frac{V_m^o}{\sigma_m^o} \quad (6.8)$$

is a standardised residual with mean zero and variance 1. Changes in $\sigma_m$ over time reflect changes in within-group wage inequality.

Likewise, we can rewrite the equation for female workers using the male wage structure as:

$$W_f^o = X_f^o \, \beta_m^o + \sigma_m^o \theta_f^o \qquad (6.9)$$

where

$$\theta_f^o = \frac{X_f^o ( \beta_f^o - \beta_m^o ) + V_f^o}{\sigma_m^o} \qquad (6.10)$$

With this notation, the average wage gap at a time 0 can be written as:

$$\overline{\Delta W^o} = \overline{\Delta X^o} \, \beta_m^o + \sigma_m^o \overline{\Delta \theta^o} \qquad (6.11)$$

where the first term reflects the predicted movement in wages and the second term reflects the residual component. The change in the male–female wage gap between two time periods can now be written as:

$$\overline{\Delta W^1} - \overline{\Delta W^o} = ( \overline{\Delta X^1} - \overline{\Delta X^o} ) \beta_m^0 + \overline{\Delta X^1} ( \beta_m^1 - \beta_m^o ) + ( \Delta Z^1 - \Delta Z^0 )$$
$$+ ( \overline{\Delta \theta^1} - \overline{\Delta \theta^o} ) \sigma_m^0 + \overline{\Delta \theta^1} ( \sigma_m^1 - \sigma_m^o ) \qquad (6.12)$$

The first three terms on the right-hand side of equation (6.12) are the same as the first two terms in equation (6.6) while the last two terms reflect our decomposition of the residual component. The fourth term captures changes in the relative positions of males and females in the conditional wage distribution. As with JMP and Blau and Kahn, we call this the "gap effect"; it measures the change in the wage gap which would occur if inequality remained the same and only the relative positions within the distribution changed. The fifth term captures the effect of changes in inequality on the wage gap holding fixed the relative male and female positions within the distribution. If women tended to be located at the lower end of the distribution, an increase in $\sigma_m$ will hurt them relative to the average male worker. The first and fourth terms are the gender-specific contributions to the changing wage gap, while the second and the fifth capture the impact of a changing wage structure on the average male–female differential. If incomes policies were reducing the wage gap we would expect it to work through the second term (by reducing $\beta$, the observed skill premium) or through the fourth term (by reducing $\sigma$ the unobserved skill premium).

The empirical calculation of the fourth and fifth terms merits further discussion. The basic premise behind this approach is that one can identify a "male comparable" for female workers in terms of both observed and unobserved characteristics and that the same forces will determine both the wage of a female worker and her comparable male worker. To find the comparable male worker, we assign each woman in cohort 1 a percentile number based on the ranking of her wage residual ($\theta_f$) in the distribution of male residuals. For instance if the median female in year 1 corresponds to the $p^{th}$ percentile of the male residual distribution, her comparable male worker would be the $p^{th}$ percentile male. The final two terms in (6.12) can both be thought of in terms of this comparable male worker. The fourth term, the gap effect, captures how the comparable male worker has changed over time. To continue with our example, we use the male residual distribution for *cohort 0* to find where the $p^{th}$ percentile male worker is. We then compare this number with the *actual median female residual* in period 0. The average of these differences across female workers is called the gap effect. Since we are using the year 0 distribution for both computations, the difference reflects the movement of women up or down a stationary distribution. Clearly, if women's positions within the male residual distribution remain unchanged over time, then the gap effect will be zero. If, however, women have improved over time, then the gap effect will contribute to a fall in the male–female wage gap. Such a change can reflect either a reduction in market discrimination or a convergence in unobservable skills.

The fifth term, the unobservable price effect, keeps the comparable worker fixed and examines how this worker fared over time as a result of changes in the residual distribution. Again continuing with our example, we know that the comparable male corresponding to the median female in period 1 is the $p^{th}$ percentile male. To calculate the unobservable price effect we compare the $p^{th}$ percentile of the male distribution in period 0 to where the actual median female worker is in period 1. Since we are holding the position in both distributions fixed (at the $p^{th}$ percentile) and allowing the distributions to change, the average of these differences reflect gains or losses suffered by females as a result of changes in within-group inequality. We measure this as changes in σ, the money value of the per unit difference in the standardised residual. In keeping with previous work, we call this the unobservable price effect.

*Chapter 7*

# Wage Differentials and Labour Market Participation

## 7.1 INTRODUCTION

There are several reasons for analysing the determinants of the participation in the labour market of men and women in the context of an analysis of male–female wage differentials. These are outlined in Section 7.2, in order to establish the aspects of the participation decision that are most relevant to explaining wage differentials. The existing literature, Irish and international, on the labour supply of men and women is then reviewed in Section 7.3. The participation decisions of men and women are then analysed using 1994 *Living in Ireland Survey* data; these results are discussed in Section 7.4. Finally, Section 7.5 addresses issues relating to unobservable characteristics of women in the labour market, and draws some conclusions about the implications of these characteristics for future patterns of wage differentials.

## 7.2 WHY STUDY PARTICIPATION DECISIONS?

One of the main explanations for the observed gap between men's and women's wages is that, on average, women in the labour market have less accumulated labour market experience. Thus, if we are to understand why male and female wages differ, we must understand more about the factors which lead to differences in levels and patterns of labour market participation.

We have seen in earlier chapters that differences in labour market experience between men and women remain an important factor underlying observed differences in wage gaps; and that changes in the observed wage gap between 1987 and 1994 may also be related to changes in patterns of labour market participation over the period.

Women are much more likely than men to withdraw from the paid labour market, or reduce their participation from full-time to part-time, during the childbearing and child-rearing years. One aspect of the study of differences in male and female labour market participation is to analyse the effects of the presence of children in the household on the labour force participation of men and women, using this to estimate the effect of having children on the amount of experience in the labour market of the typical man and woman. But other aspects of the labour participation decision are also of interest, apart from the effect of childrearing. Most obviously, wage rates in Ireland have been increasing with rising levels of education amongst both men and women, and this is likely to affect the participation decision, and hence, ultimately, feed back into wage differentials.

A further aspect of the relationship between the participation of women in the labour force and the male–female wage differential is that the composition of the group of women who leave the labour force whilst rearing their children also affects the size of the "gross", or total, differential. Thus, if the women who tend to continue to participate after having children are also those who are the most qualified or the most motivated, then the differential participation rates will to some extent *close* the gross wage gap between men and women. This will also be true if, of those who leave for childrearing, the most qualified or motivated are the first to return to work. On the other hand, if it is women who are less qualified who tend to continue to work once they have children, or to re-enter the workforce most readily afterwards, then the gross difference in wage rates between men and women will be widened.

Finally, the male–female wage differential may also be affected by the extent of part-time working if such part-time work attracts a lower hourly wage than corresponding full-time work. Married women tend to work part-time to a greater extent than others, over half of Irish part-timers being married women in 1997, even though they comprised less than one-fifth of the labour force.

Hence, wage differentials between men and women will be widened if part-time workers tend to be paid lower rates (for given human capital attributes) than their full-time counterparts. Thus, the labour supply decision as to whether to work part-time or full-time may also be relevant to the size of wage differentials. This issue is investigated in Section 7.5.

### 7.3 EXISTING EVIDENCE

It is useful to review the existing literature, both Irish and international, on the factors that determine the participation of men and women in the labour force. The first point that should be made is that the labour market behaviour of single women is usually regarded as being much more similar to that of males than that of married women. Thus, the labour supply of married women will be discussed separately here. The participation of married women in the labour market is often cited as being more sensitive to the wage rate than that of any other group, and it is usually found that women's participation and hours of work increase as wage rates increase. The standard measure of responsiveness is in terms of elasticities, e.g. a wage elasticity of labour supply of 1 indicates that a 10 per cent increase in wages would give rise to a 10 per cent increase in desired hours of work. Estimates of the elasticity of hours of work with respect to the wage rate vary widely, but typical estimates from the international literature (c.f. Killingsworth, 1983; Blundell, 1992) indicate that hours increase by between 1 per cent and 7 per cent when wages increase by 10 per cent, with most of that effect coming from non-participants beginning to participate. Estimates produced by Mroz (1987) suggest that when the sensitivity of reported results to changes in specification are taken into account, the best estimated elasticities are those at the lower end of the 1 per cent to 7 per cent range. Studies based on Irish data also show a range of possible elasticities for the labour supply of married women, depending on the methods used. Callan and Farrell (1991), using a standard method, found a high elasticity of participation with respect to the wage rate of married Irish women, a 10 per cent increase in wages leading to an increase in the participation rate of 15 per cent (equivalent to about 3 percentage points), whilst the elasticity of hours of work is small, and slightly negative, a 10 per cent wage rate increase leading to a reduction in hours worked of less than 1 per cent. Callan and van Soest (1996), using a more elaborate model, found a smaller elasticity of participation (a 1 per cent rise in wage rates leading to a rise in participation of about 0.7 percentage points), but with greater responsiveness of hours worked (a 1 per cent rise in wage rates leading to a 0.7 per cent increase in average hours worked).

Men are typically found to be less responsive in their labour market behaviour to changes in the wage rate than women. This is at least partly because most men work full-time, so that the way they can react to wage rate changes is limited to changes in their hours of work, which may not be possible for institutional reasons; moreover, men who do not work usually do not choose not to work, but are constrained by unemployment to that situation. Elasticities of hours of work with respect to the wage rate are typically found to be small and negative; results range from a 3 per cent decrease to a 0.3 per cent increase in hours worked in response to a 10 per cent increase in the wage rate. In the Irish case, Callan and Farrell (1991) report a prediction of a decrease of over 1 per cent in hours of work in response to such a wage increase; while Callan and van Soest (1996) report that a 1 per cent increase in wage rates could lead to a rise in average hours worked of 0.15 per cent. On either estimate, the labour supply of married Irish men is much less responsive to wage rates than that of married women, a result which is in line with findings in many other countries.

All of these results suggest that as wages continue to increase with higher levels of education, increasing numbers of women will participate in the labour market after they have married, whereas there will be no such increase for men. This will reduce the differential between men and women in absences from the labour market and, to the extent that the wage gap is caused by the fact that women tend to have intermittent labour market participation, could be expected in the longer term to decrease the gap between male and female wages. There could, of course, be countervailing influences on the observed wage gap from the fact that some of those drawn into the labour market as participation increases would themselves have low levels of labour market experience; but in the longer run, greater attachment to the labour market during the childbearing and child-rearing years could be expected to raise the female-to-male wage ratio.

Apart from responsiveness to changes in the wage rate, the major difference between men and women in the factors that determine their labour supply is in the effects of children. Women are invariably found to be less likely to participate when they have children, and particularly when those children are young. Thus, Callan and Farrell's (1991) study indicates that the presence of a child of up to four years old reduces the probability of participation by about 20 per cent; the total number of children also has a negative effect on participation, although the effect here is smaller. These results are fairly typical of those usually found in the international literature.

On the other hand, men appear to be less affected by the presence of children in the household; in fact, in most studies, this variable is not included in the analysis. Where it is included, the results usually show that men with more children work longer hours (Pencavel, 1986). This result is usually interpreted as indicating that, rather than being a constraint on a man's labour market behaviour, as is the case for women, having children indicates the presence of characteristics such as stability and motivation that cause men to have higher hours of work. The only results on this aspect of male labour supply in the Irish case are indirect; Murphy and Walsh (1996) find that men who have more than 5 children are more likely to be unemployed. Their suggested explanation of this result is that unemployment benefits, and hence the replacement ratio, increase with the number of children.

Work by Doris (1998), using the 1987 ESRI data, addresses the subject of why women choose to work part-time as opposed to full-time. The findings here indicate that children have a stronger negative effect on the probability of working full-time than on the probability of working part-time, a point which is clearly relevant to the size of the wage gap. Moreover, for women who are participating, those who have spent more years out of the labour market are more likely to work part-time, which accords with the perception that part-time work is used as a way to re-enter the labour market after an absence for child-rearing. Finally, the occupation with which a woman is associated is important, with part-time work more likely for women in the service sector and less likely for those working in production. This latter point is relevant to the persistence of wage differentials if part-timers are paid a lower wage, since service sector occupations have been growing faster than others in recent years.

### 7.4 ANALYSIS OF THE PARTICIPATION DECISION

The main focus of the empirical work presented here is on the differences between women and men in the factors affecting the participation decision. To this end, separate models are estimated for men and women, and the results compared.

The data used here are again drawn from the 1994 *Living in Ireland Survey*. The sample used in this chapter excludes those aged under 22 years of age, in order to avoid the complication of those in full-time education being treated as non-participants. Men over 65 and women over 60 are excluded to avoid including retirement in the non-participation category. Disabled and ill individuals are not included. Farmers and the self-employed and their spouses are also excluded, as are relatives assisting, because of the difficulty of obtaining accurate income data for these groups. Finally, employees whose occupation is farming are excluded because of the large number who were earning such low wages and working such long hours that it seemed likely that they were also receiving food and board, which would distort the wage data.

Tables 7.1 and 7.2 report the preferred models of participation for men and women respectively. In each of these models, the dependent variable is defined as equal to one if the individual is working, or not working but "seeking work". The term "seeking work" indicates that the individual is both available to take up work within two weeks and has taken steps within the previous four weeks to find work.

Each table reports the effect of the "predicted log hourly wage" on the probability of participation. The predicted wages are obtained from the regressions reported in Appendix 7.1. The prediction of wages is necessary for those who are not working and who do not, therefore, report a wage rate in the survey.

Table 7.1 shows that the probability of participation of women also is higher the greater the hourly wage, although the relationship is not linear. Theory predicts that the probability of participation increases with the wage that may be obtained in the labour market, since the higher the market wage, the more likely it is to exceed the reservation wage. Including the square of the wage allows for the possibility that the participation probability does not rise at a constant rate as wages rise. In this case, the wage rate at which the probability of participation begins to fall is at a wage of £69 per hour, a wage rate that is well beyond the maximum observed in the sample, so the participation probability increases in the wage rate over the relevant range, as theory predicts.

*Table 7.1: Probit Model of Women's Participation*

| Variable | Coefficient | t-Statistic | Marginal Effect |
|---|---|---|---|
| Predicted log hourly wage | 2.9149 | 6.95 | 1.153 |
| (Predicted log hourly wage)$^2$ | −0.3441 | −2.52 | −0.136 |
| Husband's net income (excluding means-tested benefits) | −0.0011 | −4.64 | −0.000 |
| Husband unemployed | −0.2240 | −2.14 | −0.089 |
| Age | −0.0603 | −17.27 | −0.024 |
| Number of Children Aged 0–4 | −0.5953 | −10.14 | −0.235 |
| Number of Children Aged 5–12 | −0.1862 | −5.06 | −0.074 |
| Number of Children Aged 13–18 | 0.1190 | 2.88 | 0.047 |
| Urban Dweller | 0.0960 | 1.47 | 0.038 |
| Constant | −0.4906 | −1.45 | |
| Dependent variable: Working or seeking work | | | |
| Number of observations: 2,360 | | | |
| Log likelihood: −1039.98          Pseudo $R^2$=0.364 | | | |

Another variable increasing the probability of participation is the number of children aged 13–18; this latter result is interesting, as children are more commonly observed to have negative effects on participation, with the effect decreasing with the age of the children, and possibly becoming insignificantly different from zero for children in older age groups.

Such results suggest that there are two effects of children on the decision to work for women. Firstly, as children get older, they spend more time in school and therefore need fewer hours of childcare where both parents work, so the negative effect of children on the probability of the mother participating becomes smaller as they get older. Secondly, children cost money to rear, a fact which increases the probability of participation of their parents; this "income" effect is likely to increase as children get older. These two effects, working in opposite directions, explain why older children can have a small negative effect, no effect, or even a small positive effect on the probability of participation; the latter will occur if the "income" effect of children begins to dominate the "cost of childcare" effect, and this explains the result reported in Table 7.1.

As to the other children variables, the marginal effect of the number of pre-school children is large, each pre-school child reducing the probability of participation by 24 percentage points. Each child aged between 5 and 12 also reduces the probability of participation, but by a substantially lower 7 points.

Other results show that having a husband who is unemployed reduces the probability of participation by 9 points, a very large effect. This probably reflects the importance of unobservable characteristics that are shared by husbands and wives; men who are unemployed tend to have unfavourable labour market characteristics, both observed and unobserved, and similarities in these characteristics between husbands and wives imply that their wives will have characteristics that make them less likely to participate. Alternatively, the negative effect may capture the effect of the local labour market to which both spouses are exposed, or the effect of the means testing of benefits on the incentives of the wives of the unemployed.[1]

The effect of the husband's net income, either from employment, property income or non-means-tested benefits, is negative and significant, but very small. Each year of age of the woman

---

[1] There is a growing literature on this issue; for a discussion of the evidence for the UK see Cooke, 1987; Davies et al., 1992.

reduces the probability of participation by over two points. Finally, living in an urban area increases the probability of participation, although this effect is only marginally significant.

Table 7.2 shows that for men, as for women, the probability of participation increases with higher wages, but at a decreasing rate. Here, the participation probability begins to decrease with wages at an hourly wage of £36.11; this is just within the sample range, four men in the sample having hourly wages higher than this. Although, from theory, we would expect the participation probability to be increasing in the wage rate over the entire sample range, the fact that so few men have such high wages means that this result is less problematic.

*Table 7.2: Probit Model of Men's Participation*

| Variable | Coefficient | t-Statistic | Marginal Effect |
|---|---|---|---|
| Predicted log hourly wage | 3.6829 | 4.61 | 0.564 |
| (Predicted log hourly wage)$^2$ | −0.5134 | −2.40 | −0.079 |
| Age spline: Age up to 55 | −0.0425 | −8.23 | −0.007 |
| Age over 55 | −0.1708 | −9.29 | −0.026 |
| 3 or 4 Children under 18 | −0.2951 | −2.49 | −0.052 |
| 5 or more Children under 18 | −0.6332 | −3.13 | −0.141 |
| Urban Dweller | −0.1396 | −1.76 | −0.021 |
| Married | 0.1849 | 1.66 | 0.030 |
| Constant | −1.7953 | −2.61 | |
| Dependent Variable: Working or seeking work | | | |
| Number of observations: 2304 | | | |
| Log likelihood: −672.81 Pseudo $R^2$=0.277 | | | |

The direct comparison of the effect of the wage rate on the probability of participation for men and women is made difficult by the quadratic functional form used. To solve this difficulty, elasticities of participation may be calculated for both groups by simulating the effect on the participation rate of the wage increasing by 1 per cent.

For men, the response to such an increase is a 0.31 per cent rise in the participation rate, i.e. an elasticity of participation of 0.31, a result that is somewhat higher than the elasticity of 0.23 estimated by Callan and Farrell using 1987 data. The corresponding response for women is a 0.91 per cent rise in the participation rate. These results support the usual finding that women's participation is more elastic than men's. It is notable, however, that the present estimate of female elasticity of 0.91 is lower than that estimated for married women by Callan and Farrell of 2.73. Apart from the fact that the elasticity of participation with respect to the wage rate is usually found to be higher for married women than for single women, and hence than for women in general, this result is further explained by the sharp increase in the participation of women between 1987 and 1994; a 0.9 per cent increase in the participation rate from the relatively high 1994 base entails a larger increase in the participation rate than a similar percentage increase from the lower 1987 base would have.

Having a relatively high number of dependent children — more than two — reduces the probability of men's participation significantly. As will be seen in Table 7.3, the ages of children is not important in determining the size of the negative effect for men; this leads to the conclusion that it is not because of childcare costs that the negative effect arises, as was clearly the case for women. A more plausible explanation is that a man with more children has a higher benefit replacement ratio, which creates a disincentive to participate in the labour market.

For men aged up to 55, each extra year reduces their probability of participation by less than 1 percentage point, but beyond 55, each extra year reduces the probability of participation by almost 3 points, a result that reflects early retirement options. Living in an urban area reduces the probability of participation by 2 percentage points, although this result is significant only at the 10 per cent confidence level. For men, marriage has a marginally significant positive effect on the participation probability, a result that may be due to unobservable characteristics such as stability that are reflected in being married, although a negative effect due to dependent wives increasing benefit entitlements and hence the benefit replacement ratio might also be expected here.

Table 7.3 shows the results of using identical specifications for both men and women in modelling the participation decision. This table is useful for the direct comparison of variables' effects. Several interesting points arise. Firstly, as mentioned above, the age of dependent children does not appear to affect the size of the reduction in the probability of men's participation. The hypothesis that the effect of pre-school children is the same as the effect of children aged 5–12 fails to be rejected for men, whereas it is firmly rejected for women.

Other differences indicate that a spouse's income is irrelevant to the decision to participate for men, but has a significant, albeit small, effect on women's participation decisions. Also, married men are more likely to participate in the labour market than single men, whereas for women, marriage is unimportant; clearly, it is child-rearing responsibilities and not marriage *per se* that drive differences in participation rates between men and women. Note that the "spouse unemployed" variable which was shown to be significant for the labour supply of women in Table 7.1, could not be used in the model of men's participation because of the small number of men who had an unemployed wife, and hence was omitted from both specifications to ensure comparability.

It is possible to use the results from Table 7.3 to calculate the cumulative impact on labour market experience of having children, in order to illustrate the differences between men and women in their importance.[2]

These calculations do not take account of the fact that as children get older, so do their parents, even though the results show that the age of the individual also plays a role in determining participation patterns. Nonetheless, it is interesting to isolate the effect of children on participation. The calculations show that for a typical woman, having two children will entail a total reduction in experience of 3 years and 4 months, whereas for a man, having

---

[2] The marginal effects of children of different ages on the participation probabilities of an individual with no children but with average values of other variables are used in these calculations; each child's effect on lifetime experience is (marginal effect of number of children aged 0-4)×5 plus (marginal effect of number of children aged 5-12)×8 plus (marginal effect of number of children aged 13-18)×6. Multiplying by two gives an estimate of the effect of two children on labour market experience.

two children reduces total experience by less than 6 months. As mentioned above, the reason for the reduction in experience of men is related to the effect of the number of children on the benefit replacement ratio.

*Table 7.3: Comparable Probit Models of Participation for Men and Women*

| Variable | Men | | Women | |
|---|---|---|---|---|
| | *Coefficient* | *t-Statistic* | *Coefficient* | *t-Statistic* |
| Predicted log hourly wage | 3.6474 | 4.49 | 2.9860 | 7.12 |
| (Predicted log hourly wage)$^2$ | −0.4939 | −2.28 | −0.3672 | −2.69 |
| Spouse's net income (except means-tested benefits) | −0.0001 | −0.09 | −0.0009 | −3.66 |
| Age | 0.0476 | 1.71 | −0.0059 | −0.20 |
| (Age)$^2$ | −0.0013 | −4.14 | −0.0007 | −1.86 |
| Number of Children Aged 0–4 | −0.1873 | −2.20 | −0.6160 | −10.15 |
| Number of Children Aged 5–12 | −0.1561 | −3.01 | −0.2304 | −5.76 |
| Number of Children Aged 13–18 | 0.0018 | 0.03 | 0.0852 | 1.98 |
| Urban Dweller | −0.1499 | −1.88 | 0.0968 | 1.48 |
| Married | 0.2718 | 2.12 | −0.0336 | −0.33 |
| Constant | −3.2122 | −4.14 | −1.5327 | −2.42 |
| Dependent variable: Working or seeking work | | | | |
| Number of observations | 2,292[3] | | 2,360 | |
| Pseudo R$^2$ | 0.268 | | 0.363 | |
| Log Likelihood | −679.61 | | −1040.54 | |

---

[3] The difference in the number of observations between this model and that reported in Table 2 is due to a number of these men not reporting their spouses' net income.

The models reported in Table 7.3 may also be used to illustrate the differences in the time paths of accumulated experience between men and women. Figure 7.1 plots years of experience against age for a "typical" man and woman. In each case, he/she is married and, beginning at age 22 with 2.4 years of experience (the sample average for both men and women at that age) goes on to have two children, one when aged 26 and the second when aged 29. Again, for other variables, the sample means (for men or women, as appropriate) are used, a simplification that is clearly unrealistic in the case of the wage rate, given the evidence presented in earlier chapters, and indeed in the appendix to the present chapter, that labour market experience increases the wage rate. This limitation should be borne in mind when examining Figure 7.1.

***Figure 7.1. Cumulative Experience Predicted for a Typical Married Man and Woman with Two Children, by Age***

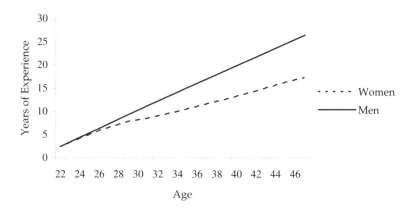

The figure shows that the divergence in experience in the labour market between men and women begins to emerge clearly at around age 29, when the second child is born. At this time, with two children aged under four in the household, the participation probability predicted by the model is 0.38 for a woman, and 0.97 for a man; moreover, the negative effect of children is reinforced more by increasing age for women than for men.[4] By the time the second child is 18, there is a nine-year difference in experience between men and women.

## 7.5 UNOBSERVABLE CHARACTERISTICS

Having discussed the effects of wage rates and children on the participation rates of men and women, and hence on accumulated experience in the labour market, we now turn to the other issues raised in Section 7.2.

### Selection Bias Issues

The first of these is the issue of whether the low participation rate of married women in the labour market compared to that of men may reduce the gross male–female wage differential to the extent that it is those women who are most motivated, and hence who have characteristics which are unobservable but which tend to increase the wage rate received, that are working at present. If this were the case, then as extra women begin to participate in the labour market, these unobservables will become, on average, less favourable for market wage rates. Clearly, since we are discussing unobservable characteristics, these cannot be explicitly modelled. Nonetheless, the econometric model used in estimating the wage rate for women (reported in Table A.7.2 in the Appendix to this chapter) may be used to shed some light on this matter.

The model referred to — Heckman's Selection Bias-Corrected model — explicitly takes account of the fact that those who report wage rates in the survey are currently participating in the labour market and hence may have favourable unobservable characteristics that increase the wage rate, and that this implies that estimating a wage equation as though these women were representative of non-working individuals will yield biased estimates of the wage equation. In this model, as proposed by Heckman (1980), estimated parameters from a model of participation are used to

---

[4] Note that although the probability of participation is initially increasing in age for men, the maximum of the quadratic relationship is at age 18, so the relationship between age and participation is negative over the relevant range, albeit only slightly so at low ages.

calculate a quantity known as the "inverse Mills' ratio", $\lambda_i$, and this is then included as a variable in a wage equation to take account of the possibility that those working are not representative of the whole population. If the coefficient on $\lambda_i$ is positive and significantly different from zero, this indicates that those participating do indeed have unobservable characteristics that positively affect their wage rates. An examination of the results in Table A.7.2 shows that the coefficient on $\lambda_i$ is positive and significant, which supports the view that unobservable characteristics are raising women's wages above what they would be if currently participating women had the population average of these characteristics. This means that as participation increases in the future, the composition of the new participants will reduce the positive effect of increased experience on wage rates to some extent.

Thus, as has been indicated above, whilst the effect of increased experience of women in the labour force will be to reduce the wage gap in the long term, it is acknowledged that, in the shorter term, the fact that new participants have low levels of experience on average will temporarily increase the wage gap. This conclusion was reached even without taking the unobservable characteristics of non-participants, who form the pool of potential re-entrants, into account; the fact that new participants have unobservable characteristics that are unfavourable, on average, will further act to widen the wage gap.

The importance of unobservables also has implications for the interpretation of the decomposition of the wage gap carried out in Chapter 3. If the unobservable characteristics of new participants acts to increase the wage gap beyond what it would be in the absence of differences in unobservables, then we should expect to see more of the wage gap being attributed to unobservable factors as participation increases. Since the unexplained portion of the wage gap is often taken as an indicator of the extent of discrimination, this point indicates further caution either in using the "unexplained" portion of the wage gap as a measure of discrimination, because it also includes differences in unobservables; or in using changes in the unexplained part of the wage gap over time as a measure of whether discrimination is increasing or decreasing, particularly at a time when participation is expanding rapidly. In fact, if women who entered the labour market between

1987 and 1994 had more unfavourable unobservable characteristics, on average, than women already participating in 1987, we would expect to see the unexplained portion of the wage gap increasing.[5] The fact that it actually decreased according to the analysis in Chapter 3 suggests that the factors reducing it were even stronger than ultimately recorded.

## Part-time Working

A further issue raised in Section 7.2 concerned the effect of part-time working on wage differentials; this is an issue that also turns out to revolve around the importance of unobservable characteristics, and for this reason it is included in this section. It is sometimes argued that the growth in part-time work that has occurred in many countries in recent years is detrimental to the narrowing of wage differentials between men and women, on the grounds that, firstly, part-time jobs pay less than equivalent full-time jobs; and, secondly, part-time jobs are held primarily by women. It is certainly true that women work part-time to a much greater extent than men. Thus, in the present survey, 32 per cent of women work part-time, compared to just 8 per cent of men; 71 per cent of part-timers are women although they make up only 40 per cent of workers in the sample. As to whether they are paid less than full-timers, the evidence in the current survey is less clear. The average hourly wage for part-timers in the present sample is £6.64, compared to £6.77 for full-timers; part-timers do earn less, but the difference in the averages is not statistically significant. If, however, teachers are excluded from the sample, the average part-time wage drops to £4.91 per hour, compared to £6.37 per hour for full-timers, a difference that is significant.[6]

The issue as to why part-timers might be paid a lower wage than full-timers requires some thought. Two quite different rea-

---

[5] No analysis of the effect of unobservables on the wage gap was undertaken in the 1994 study based on 1987 data, so we cannot say for certain that the same selectivity issue arose for those not participating in 1987. However, it is likely that the effect was in the same direction then as in 1994.

[6] This difference in results when teachers are excluded arises despite the fact that teachers are recorded as working full-time if they work more than 24 hours per week, whereas for everyone else the cut-off is 30 hours per week.

sons could be adduced. Firstly, part-timers may be inherently less "motivated" or "ambitious" than full-timers; in this case, their lower pay is due to their having less favourable unobserved characteristics than full-timers, and if part-timers were working full-time, they would not be paid a higher hourly wage. Secondly, it may be that part-timers receive a lower return to human capital than full-timers; this may be because of either higher costs of employing part-timers per hour worked, or because a high relative supply of women wishing to work part-time depresses the wage paid in jobs offered on a part-time basis. In this second pair of cases, if part-timers were to work full-time, they would earn a higher hourly wage. Of course, both these effects may be in operation at the same time.

It is clearly necessary, therefore, to take account of unobservable characteristics when examining this issue, and in particular, any differences in unobservables between part-timers and full-timers. A method for doing so has been proposed by Nakamura and Nakamura (1983), and this procedure is followed here. The essential idea behind this method is to estimate *two* terms for unobservable characteristics similar to the $\lambda_i$ discussed above, one for part-time workers, $\lambda_{PTi}$ and another for full-time workers, $\lambda_{FTi}$; the precise definitions of these variables are included in Appendix 7.2. Separate wage estimations may then be carried out for part-timers and full-timers, using $\lambda_{PTi}$ or $\lambda_{FTi}$ in the regression, as appropriate.[7] Where the coefficient on the relevant $\lambda_i$ is significant and positive, this indicates, as before, that women working in that hours regime have "good" unobservable characteristics compared to other women. Note that since this methodology controls for unobservable characteristics, any differences in the parameter estimates between the two models may be interpreted as differential returns to human capital.

The results of the wage regressions for part-time and full-time female workers are shown in Table 7.4; the small number of male part-timers precludes a similar analysis for men. Attention should be drawn to two aspects of the results. Firstly, the coefficients and t-statistics for the selection terms $\lambda_{PTi}$ and $\lambda_{FTi}$ indicate that there is

---

[7] This analysis may therefore be seen as a more detailed exploration of the likely "composition" effect of new participants on wages discussed above.

positive selection into full-time work, but not into part-time work. In other words, those working full-time in the sample have unobservable characteristics that make them both more likely to work full-time, and more likely to earn higher wages than others, whereas part-timers appear to be randomly selected from the population, so they do not have unobservable characteristics that raise their wages.

**Table 7.4: Wage Regressions for Full-time and Part-time Female Workers**

| Variable | Full-Time | | Part-Time | |
|---|---|---|---|---|
| *Variable* | *Coefficient* | *t-Statistic* | *Coefficient* | *t-Statistic* |
| Education: Group/ Inter/Junior Cert. | 0.0670 | 1.13 | 0.1870 | 2.30 |
| Leaving/Post-Leaving Cert. | 0.3649 | 6.52 | 0.3602 | 4.77 |
| Diploma | 0.5790 | 8.30 | 0.5104 | 3.41 |
| Primary/Higher Degree | 0.9646 | 15.93 | 1.4295 | 12.87 |
| Years of work experience | 0.0716 | 12.78 | 0.0408 | 3.94 |
| (Years of work experience)$^2$/100 | −0.1334 | −8.11 | −0.0644 | −2.19 |
| Years not in work | −0.0369 | −4.28 | −0.0326 | −2.86 |
| (Years not in work)$^2$/100 | 0.1034 | 3.53 | 0.0774 | 2.39 |
| $\lambda_i$ ($\lambda_{FTi}$ or $\lambda_{PTi}$) | 0.1822 | 3.44 | 0.0587 | 0.96 |
| Constant | 0.6885 | 9.08 | 1.0290 | 8.95 |
| Dependent Variable | Log Hourly Wage | | Log Hourly Wage | |
| Number of observations | 735 | | 307 | |
| $R^2$ | 0.508 | | 0.539 | |

Secondly, the coefficients on the two regressions are similar; hypothesis tests of their equality show that only for the coefficient on "educated to degree/higher degree level" is the difference significant. Interestingly, in that case, the difference is in the opposite direction to that expected — the return to third-level education appears to be greater for part-timers than for full-timers. Because most teachers have degrees, an alternative model to that reported in Table 7.4, including a dummy variable for being a teacher was estimated; the results (not reported here) show that the difference in return to third-level education disappears, indicating that this difference is due to high rates of hourly pay for teachers working part-time.[8]

Since full-timers have positive unobservable characteristics which raise their hourly wage rates above other women's, whereas part-timers do not, and since the returns to human capital are statistically indistinguishable for part-timers and full-timers (teachers apart), if women currently working part-time began to work full-time, their wage rates would not change. The conclusion may therefore be drawn that there is no evidence that the higher level of part-time working among women is contributing to the wage differential between men and women.

## 7.6 CONCLUSIONS

The evidence presented in this chapter has illustrated the importance of men's and women's different childcare responsibilities in determining the different rates of participation between men and women, and how these different participation rates explain the differences in years of labour market experience, a variable that has been shown to be important in determining wage rates in previous chapters. The issue of the importance of part-time working to wage differentials was also explored, and the conclusion drawn that differential rates of part-time working do not explain the lower wage rates of women.

---

[8] Recall that a different hours cut-off was used for teachers when constructing the part-time/full-time indicator — a weekly working time of 24 hours or more counts as full-time work for teachers whereas for everyone else, 30 hours or more comprise full-time work.

## APPENDIX 7.1 WAGE REGRESSIONS

### Table A.7.1: OLS Wage Regression for Men

| Variable | Coefficient | t-Statistic |
|---|---|---|
| Education: Group Cert. | 0.2063 | 5.44 |
| Inter./Junior Cert. | 0.3142 | 9.05 |
| Leaving/Post-Leaving Cert. | 0.4694 | 12.67 |
| Diploma | 0.6262 | 12.15 |
| Primary Degree | 0.9648 | 16.80 |
| Higher Degree | 1.0969 | 17.09 |
| Years of work experience | 0.0233 | 4.34 |
| Years not in work | −0.0188 | −2.14 |
| (Years not in work)$^2$/100 | 0.1235 | 3.55 |
| Age | 0.0543 | 5.47 |
| (Age)$^2$ | −0.0007 | −8.60 |
| Married | 0.1752 | 6.25 |
| Constant | 0.0396 | 0.22 |
| Dependent Variable: log hourly wage | | |
| Number of observations: 1586 | $R^2$=0.491 | |

*Note*: Omitted education category is "no qualifications".

## Table A.7.2: Heckman Sample Selection Bias-Corrected Wage Regression for Women

| Variable | Coefficient | t-Statistic |
|---|---|---|
| *Wage Equation* | | |
| Education: Group/Inter/Junior Cert. | 0.1343 | 2.84 |
| Leaving/Post-Leaving Cert. | 0.3753 | 8.36 |
| Diploma | 0.5685 | 9.25 |
| Primary/Higher Degree | 1.1172 | 21.01 |
| Years of work experience | 0.0619 | 11.81 |
| (Years of work experience)$^2$/100 | –0.1096 | –7.25 |
| Years not in work | –0.0273 | –4.72 |
| (Years not in work)$^2$/100 | 0.0711 | 3.62 |
| Constant | 0.7732 | 12.16 |
| $\lambda_i$ | 0.1037 | 2.59 |
| *Participation Equation* | | |
| Education: Group/Inter/Junior Cert. | 0.2445 | 2.74 |
| Leaving/Post-Leaving Cert. | 0.4276 | 4.93 |
| Diploma | 0.4243 | 2.89 |
| Primary/Higher Degree | 0.7903 | 6.07 |
| Years of work experience | 0.1115 | 9.29 |
| (Years of work experience)$^2$/100 | –0.2810 | –7.73 |
| Years not in work | –0.1362 | –13.10 |
| (Years not in work)$^2$/100 | 0.2260 | 6.93 |
| Child aged 0–4 | –0.6028 | –6.07 |
| Number of children aged 0–12 | –0.1658 | –4.45 |
| Constant | 0.0222 | 0.184 |
| Dependent Variables: Log Hourly Wage and In Work | | |
| Number of Observations: 2437 | Log Likelihood: –1642.84 | |

*Note*: Omitted education category is "no qualifications".

## APPENDIX 7.2: PARTICIPATION EQUATIONS USED TO CONSTRUCT $\lambda_{pt}$ AND $\lambda_{ft}$

*Table A.7.3: Probit Models of Participation and Working Full-time for Women*

|  | Participation | | Full-time work | |
|---|---|---|---|---|
| *Variable* | *Coefficient* | *t-Statistic* | *Coefficient* | *t-Statistic* |
| Education: Group/ Inter/Junior Cert. | 0.1886 | 2.19 | 0.2933 | 2.65 |
| Leaving/Post-Leaving Cert. | 0.2562 | 3.01 | 0.4305 | 4.09 |
| Diploma | 0.4255 | 2.63 | 0.6655 | 4.16 |
| Primary/Higher Degree | 0.6512 | 4.46 | 0.4956 | 3.73 |
| Years of work experience | 0.0767 | 6.44 | 0.0951 | 7.17 |
| (Years of work experience)$^2$/100 | −0.2380 | −6.47 | −0.2594 | −6.61 |
| Years not in work | −0.1540 | −14.05 | −0 1669 | −13.78 |
| (Years not in work)$^2$/100 | 0.2178 | 6.72 | 0.2711 | 6.58 |
| Child aged 0–4 | −0.7517 | −7.55 | −0.4705 | −4.19 |
| Number of children aged 0–12 | −0.2097 | −5.84 | −0.3804 | −8.07 |
| Constant | 1.0671 | 8.24 | −0.0189 | −0.14 |
| Dependent Variable | Participating | | Working full-time | |
| Number of observations | 2,437 | | 2,437 | |
| Log Likelihood | −1053.08 | | −870.34 | |

The above results were used to construct $\lambda_{FT}$ and $\lambda_{PT}$ as follows:

$$\lambda_{FTi} = \frac{\phi(\beta_{FT}X_i)}{\Phi(\beta_{FT}X_i)}$$

where $\phi(\cdot)$ is the standard normal density function, $\Phi(\cdot)$ is the cumulative normal, and $\beta_{FT}$ refers to the parameter estimates of the Full-time / Not Full-time model shown in Table A.7.3.

$$\lambda_{PTi} = \frac{\phi(\beta_{WK} \mathbf{X}_i) - \phi(\beta_{FT} \mathbf{X}_i)}{\Phi(\beta_{WK} \mathbf{X}_i) - \Phi(\beta_{FT} \mathbf{X}_i)}$$

where $\beta_{WK}$ are the estimated parameters from the Participation model of Table A.7.3.

*Chapter 8*

# Policy Issues

## 8.1 INTRODUCTION

Before considering how particular policies might influence the gender wage gap, we take stock (Section 8.2) of the nature of current policy objectives in the area of labour market equality between the sexes. The *Strategy Statement* of the Department of Justice, Equality and Law Reform (1998) is helpful in summarising recent official statements and situating them in an overall context, including EU directives and guidelines. While the overall objectives have now been stated more clearly and concisely than heretofore, the implications of our findings in earlier chapters, in the context of those objectives, are not clear-cut. Quite varying interpretations of the findings are possible, and the implications for practical policy issues are, in consequence, quite different.

We then consider three types of policy, each of which can be aimed at reducing the gap between men's and women's wages. Section 8.3 examines legislation designed to deal directly with issues of equal pay and discrimination. We consider how Irish legislation on this topic has changed over time, and how it compares with similar legislation in other countries. Section 8.4 deals with collective bargaining and the role of trade unions, because of their central role in wage determination. Section 8.5 returns to the subject of minimum wage legislation, drawing on results from Chapter 6. Minimum wage policy deals directly with wage inequality and although it is not generally introduced purely for reasons of gender equality, it could have significant implications for the gender wage gap. In the following two sections, we consider policies which deal more indirectly with gender inequality in the labour market — policies which aim at strengthening women's labour market attachment and reducing occupational segregation. These have been grouped into two categories based on two dimensions of inequality that current and previous research has identified as important for the wage gap:

1. Policies aimed at reducing discontinuity in women's careers (Section 8.6);

2. Strategies to reduce occupational segregation (Section 8.7).

The main themes of the chapter are drawn together in Section 8.8.

## 8.2 POLICY OBJECTIVES

### Official Statements

The *Strategy Statement 1998–2000* of the Department of Justice, Equality and Law Reform (1998) summarises recent commitments of government, including those under Partnership 2000, and the EU context of directives and guidelines under which policy is formed. The fundamental aim is stated as follows:

> To bring about a more equal society, by outlawing discrimination and by facilitating equality of opportunity, especially for certain groups that have experienced disadvantage (Department of Justice, Equality and Law Reform, 1998).

This is translated into four objectives:

1. Put in place a statutory foundation for equality, especially rights-based anti-discrimination legislation.

2. Provide a sound infrastructure to work towards the elimination of discrimination, to promote equal opportunities and provide redress for persons who have suffered discrimination contrary to employment equality or equal status legislation.

3. Develop and pursue equal opportunities policies in the areas of equal pay for like work; equal treatment and positive action measures in employment; and the equal provision of goods, services and facilities.

4.  Promote the reconciliation of work and family responsibilities.

In the context of labour market equality between the sexes, the emphasis of policy is therefore on *equality of opportunity*. This is a difficult concept to define and an even more difficult one to measure. The statistics available to us measure labour market outcomes. But while *equality of outcome* can be defined, measured and monitored more readily, this does not solve the problem of measuring and monitoring equality of opportunity.

If equality of outcome rather than equality of opportunity were the goal, then policy would have to tackle each of the causes of unequal outcomes; but then policy would offset any possible differences between the sexes in respect of preferences — for example, as between work in the labour market and caring work in the home. A focus on equality of opportunity requires greater attention to processes — such as recruitment, promotion and training — which generate labour market outcomes. But to some extent the monitoring of such processes depends on monitoring of outcomes: a process may seem non-discriminatory, but have indirect or hidden discriminatory elements which only emerge by monitoring outcomes.

## How Much Policy Intervention is Warranted?

There are quite differing views on the nature and extent of policy interventions required in order to achieve equal opportunity objectives.[1] For example, some would argue that substantial subsidies of purchased childcare are a *sine qua non* for true equality of labour market opportunity. Others would say that this is true for labour market outcomes, but that it is less clear that such subsidisation is necessary for equality of opportunity. Callan and Wren (1994) discuss this issue in some depth and conclude that there is a valid case for subsidisation on an equal opportunity basis, but that it is more subtle and less obvious than is sometimes thought.

---

[1] At an earlier stage, there were differing views of the likely impact of equal pay legislation. The "free market" view stressed the irrationality of discrimination and argued that intervention was likely to lead to job losses, particularly for women. In Ireland, growth in female employment continued apace, together with an increase in the female-to-male wage ratio.

More generally, Cain (1966) argues that economic theory does not have very convincing explanations for the persistence of discrimination. Many potential sources of discrimination would lead to discriminating firms being driven out of business by more efficient firms who do not discriminate. The more convincing explanations relate to "statistical discrimination" as discussed in Chapter 4, though even here there are some unresolved issues. But, as Cain stresses, this does not imply that discrimination cannot exist, only that further theoretical work on its underpinnings and persistence (including barriers to competition, such as barriers to entry to certain professions) is needed.

There can be very different readings of the policy implications of our findings. The fall in the unexplained wage gap to around 5 per cent can be interpreted as indicating the effectiveness of current policies in dealing with discrimination, with the remaining gap due perhaps to unobserved or unmeasured differences between men and women in terms of productivity-relevant characteristics. On this reading, current policies *are* enough to achieve the equality of opportunity objective. Differences in outcome reflect differences in productivity-relevant characteristics, some of which relate to the different preferences of men and women regarding the allocation of their time between the labour market and caring for children or other family members.

Attempts to manipulate male and female wage rates towards equality would then involve distortions in the labour market, which would introduce inefficiencies, and result in women being over-rewarded relative to their labour market characteristics. For simplicity, we could characterise this as a "free market" view. It stresses that men and women make choices regarding the extent and nature of their labour market participation which reflect the opportunities available and their own preferences, and that preferences may differ as between the average man and the average woman. It recognises that the existence of childcare costs, and the existence or level of public subsidy for childcare, will influence such choices. But there is no "correct" level of subsidisation: this is a matter of social choice and countries end up with quite different levels and structures of subsidy, with changes over time. At all times, it could be argued, individuals are free to make choices reflecting their preferences in the light of their current opportunities and childcare subsidies (which are socially and politically determined).

At the other end of the spectrum (and there are many intermediate possibilities) it could be argued that the figure of 5 per cent for the unexplained wage gap understates the true level of discrimination. Proponents of this view could argue that some of the "explained" gap relates to inequality of access to education and training courses, and to decisions regarding earlier allocation of time between the paid labour market and caring work in the home. If there is currently, or has in the past, been labour market discrimination involving lower wages for women than for men of similar characteristics, then women would rationally have decided to invest less in education and labour market time, as the rewards would have been lower. Thus some of the explained gap could represent a response to labour market discrimination currently or in the past. For example, the marriage bar did not affect simply those who were directly affected, but would have influenced the educational choices of a generation of women who grew up in a society where it was taken as the norm that women gave up employment on marriage. Furthermore, it could be argued that the unobserved characteristics of men and women are such that the "unexplained" wage gap is an underestimate of direct labour market discrimination. On this basis, the search for equality of opportunity could require significant further interventions of the types detailed below.

There is no clear way of choosing between these interpretations on the basis of existing evidence; this ambiguity applies not just to Ireland but to the interpretation of similar results for many other countries. Other evidence, including detailed micro-level study of the processes of recruitment, promotion and career progression are needed to help guide the formation of policy. In what follows, we outline the sorts of policy interventions that can be relevant to the equality of opportunity objective, drawing on Irish policy experience and policy debates, and also on the experience of other countries. The precise extent and nature of interventions to be chosen will depend not only on the results of our analyses, but on social preferences over different objectives, including economic growth, the distribution of income, and equality of opportunity.

## 8.3 EQUAL PAY AND EQUAL OPPORTUNITIES LEGISLATION

Governmental effort to promote gender equality in the Irish labour market began on the legislative route. In this section (Box 8.1) we outline the legislation enacted to deal with equal opportunities and gender discrimination in Ireland. The impact of this legislation is assessed in the context of international policy experience and evaluation studies.

### Box 8.1: *Equal Pay and Equal Opportunities Legislation in Ireland*

*Anti-Discrimination (Pay) Act, 1974, and Employment Equality Act, 1977*

Legislation on equal pay was first introduced in Ireland in the form of the *Anti-Discrimination (Pay) Act, 1974*, in response to EEC Directive 117. The Act came into effect on 1 January 1976. The Act established the right to equal pay for "like work", including work of "equal value", which was defined in terms of skill, physical or mental requirements, responsibility and working conditions. The *Employment Equality Act* was introduced in 1977 and prohibited discrimination in recruitment, training, conditions of employment and promotion opportunities on the grounds of sex or marital status. The Act also explicitly outlawed indirect discrimination (i.e. where a condition or requirement is applied equally to both sexes, but operates such that the proportion of persons disadvantaged is much higher among one sex, and the condition cannot be shown to be essential to the job). Both of the Acts were implemented through a complaint-based system. Those who believe that their rights under either Act were violated were required to bring their case to an Equality Officer or the Labour Court. Both the Equality Officers and the Employment Equality Agency[2] had the power to carry out an investigation into discrimination claims. The Employment Equality Agency was also given an information, advisory and monitoring role. (Further details of both the Acts are discussed in the earlier report by Callan and Wren (1994) and in Curtin (1989).)

---

[2] Equality Officers were appointed under the Anti-Discrimination Pay Act and the Employment Equality Agency was set up under the 1977 Employment Equality Act.

*Employment Equality Act 1998*

In June 1998, the *Employment Equality Act, 1998*, was passed, replacing the *Employment Equality Act, 1977*, and the *Anti-Discrimination (Pay) Act, 1974*. The legislation extends the grounds on which discrimination in employment is outlawed from gender and marital status alone, to include family status, sexual orientation, religion, age, disability, race and membership of the Travelling community. Many of the provisions in the new Act are identical to those in the original legislation; however, there are a number of novel elements. Firstly, the 1998 Act extends coverage to the Defence Forces for the first time. Secondly, it makes claims easier by changing the time limit from six months from the date of the *first* occurrence of the alleged discrimination to six months from the most recent occurrence. Thirdly, it defines sexual harassment for the first time in Irish law. Fourthly, and perhaps most importantly, it introduces a more proactive approach for the Employment Equality Agency, which has been reconstituted as the *Equality Authority*. The Equality Authority can now request businesses with over 50 employees to conduct *equality reviews* and prepare *equality action plans* or if appropriate to carry out such a review and prepare an action plan itself. Businesses failing to implement the provisions of an equality action plan will be issued with substantive notice, which can be enforced by the Courts. The Equality Authority has also been empowered to draw up codes of practice to eliminate discrimination and promote equal opportunities, which can be given statutory effect by the Minister for Justice, Equality and Law Reform.

Two types of legislation are considered, equal pay policies and those dealing with equal opportunities. The latter type of legislation is expected to have an indirect effect on wage inequality by eliminating discrimination in processes such as training, hiring, and promotion. Equality in access to training, jobs and promotion opportunities is crucial to the task of reducing the segregation of men and women into different occupations (horizontal segregation) and into different levels within occupations (vertical segregation). Therefore, equal opportunities legislation can help reduce the "unexplained" variation in the wage gap that is often attributed to discrimination, and can decrease the levels of gender segregation in the labour market, which is commonly seen as a major source of wage variation between men and women.

## Impact of Equal Pay Legislation

It is still too early to evaluate the impact of the 1998 changes in the legislation on gender differences in wage levels. However, information on the evolution of the male–female wage gap following the earlier legislation together with research experiences in other countries can provide an insight into the role that legislation can play in reducing wage inequalities. As mentioned in Chapter 1, Callan and Wren's analysis of trends in hourly wages of manual workers in the manufacturing industry in Ireland suggests that the original legislation is likely to have played a role in raising female wages more rapidly than men's in subsequent years (1994: 5). The female-to-male wage ratio increased significantly for this group of workers in the late 1970s, which coincided with the implementation of the Anti-Discrimination (Pay) Act and the first Employment Equality Act. A similar trend emerged in the UK for the same time period, which led Zabalza and Tzannatos (1985) to conclude that anti-discriminatory legislation had a positive effect on relative earnings and relative employment for women in the UK. Hakim (1992) also argues that the British equal opportunities legislation had a significant impact on the level of gender segregation in the labour market.

It would be unwise, however, to attribute all of the improvement in Irish wage ratios to the introduction of equality legislation, when many other changes in the Irish economy and society were occurring at the same time, including changes in social attitudes, rising levels of female education and the growth of service sector employment. The results of international studies also caution against attributing too large a role to legislation alone in reducing gender wage differentials. For example, in a study of 13 OECD countries, Whitehouse (1992: 75) found no association between the initiation of equal pay and equal opportunities legislation and the female-to-male wage ratio. This does not mean legislation is inherently ineffective but that its results are dependent upon the wider context in which the legislation operates.

Previous research suggests that the system of implementation and definitions of equality are crucial to the effectiveness of anti-discrimination laws. Early definitions of "like work" were limited to those carrying out the same jobs. While this could eliminate the blatant discrimination involved in separate wage rates for men and women doing the same job,[3] the segregation of men and women into different occupations in the workforce meant that this definition is severely limited in its application. As mentioned already, the Irish legislation includes provision of equal pay for work of equal value, which extends coverage to those in different occupations working for the same employer, who exercise the same level of skill, mental or physical effort, and responsibility in their jobs and work in the same conditions.

Applying this legal guarantee has proved difficult in many countries, because of the problems of quantifying the value of work and overturning inherent gender biases in skill definitions (Phillips and Taylor, 1980; Jenson, 1989).[4] The Employment Equality Act, 1998, does not refer to any formal job evaluation schemes that would allow comparisons across very different jobs. However, both the European Commission (1994) and ICTU (1987) provide guidelines for setting up, applying and reviewing job classification schemes. Both documents stress the importance of including a range of job features/demands which capture the content of both predominantly male and predominantly female jobs so that both can be evaluated using a common standard. They also emphasise the need to give due credit to traditionally female skills such as caring, human relations skills, and manual dexterity. Nevertheless, there is still considerable debate on how jobs should be evaluated, who should be involved in the evaluation process and how the results should be incorporated into payment systems (e.g. see Gunderson, 1989). The difficulty in establishing equal value has meant that few cases involving very different occupations have been taken in Ireland.

---

[3] This type of discrimination was more widespread in the late 1960s and early 1970s and in some countries (for example, Australia) was formalised in central wage bargaining systems (Kidd and Shannon, 1996). In Ireland, the early National Wage Agreements (NWA) included unequal rates of pay for men and women doing the same job. For example, the 1970 NWA specified that women should get 85 per cent of the Phase 1 settlement. This differential was gradually reduced in subsequent agreements (O'Brien, 1981: Appendix A).

[4] The existing levels of responsibility of different groups can also reflect differences in promotion opportunities, which are also structured by gender.

The limitation of the law to within-establishment comparisons means that its capacity to reduce wage differentials that arise through segregation is severely restricted and the economy-wide effects of court rulings are small. This limitation is shared with most European and US equal pay legislation.[5] The rules governing the implementation of equal pay legislation have proved to be decisive in determining the law's effectiveness. In general, complaint-driven approaches appear to be less effective than those where class actions are taken or where a government inspectorate proactively ensures compliance (Gunderson, 1989). The affirmative action programmes operating in the United States place the burden of proof onto the employer. Since 1968, Federal contractors are required to implement affirmative action plans in relation to their hiring and promotion practices (see Box 8.2). However, the quota systems used to achieve these ends have been controversial and are seen to be incompatible with EU legislation (see Box 8.3).

Although the Irish law is complaints-driven, the representation of complainants by trade unions means that a large group of women can be involved in the same action. Furthermore, the laws grant considerable enforcement powers for the Equality Authority (formerly the Employment Equality Agency). Curtin (1989) argues that these powers have not been fully utilised in the past because of lack of resources. It remains to be seen, therefore, to what extent the enhanced power granted under the 1998 Employment Equality Act will be applied.

This discussion suggests that the potential for further reductions in the gender wage gap through equal pay and equal opportunities-type legislation is limited in a number of respects. Previous research suggests that the greatest limitation is the inability to make comparison across establishments and the difficulties in establishing "equal value" across very different types of jobs. Direct discrimination in terms of different pay for the same job is becoming increasingly rare, and the analysis above has shown that the

---

[5] One exception is Ontario's Pay Equity Act, 1987, which requires all employers to adjust their wage systems on the basis of comparable worth evaluations. This increases the potential impact of rulings dramatically; however, the ultimate impact will depend on the enforcement of this law.

amount of unexplained variance in men's and women's wages that cannot be attributed to human capital differences has decreased since 1987; therefore, it cannot be expected that the new legislation will have as large an impact as the earlier laws.

## Box 8.2: US Legislation on Equality

*Equal Pay Act, 1963*

Requires equal pay for work of equal skill, effort, responsibility, and working conditions. "It does not allow comparisons across jobs of different content, and hence it does not entail the comparable worth concept" (Gunderson, 1989: 56).

*Title VII of the Civil Rights Act of 1964*

Prohibits employment and wage discrimination on the grounds of race, religion, national origin and sex. Set up Equal Employment Opportunities Commission (EEOC) which had investigative powers but no enforcement authority. The 1972 Equal Opportunity Act gave the EEOC authority to bring its own legal actions; this included class suits such as the nation-wide suit against the steel industry in 1974 covering over 700,000 employees. Through interpretation of the law (e.g. *Griggs* v *Duke Power Co.*), the definition of discrimination was extended to cover "unnecessary practices that were neutral on their face but were discriminatory in effect" (Rose, 1994). This led to a focus on unequal outcomes as well as unequal opportunities.

*Equal Employment Opportunity Act, 1972*

Amended the 1964 Act. Aimed to improve administration and effectiveness of Title VII and extended coverage to government employees (local, state and federal).

*Executive Order No. 11, 246, 1965.*

Prohibited discrimination by race (and, later, sex) among organisations fulfilling government contracts or sub-contracts. The order was enforced through the Office of Federal Contract Compliance (OFCC). In 1968, the OFCC required contractors to prepare affirmative action plans to eliminate "underutilization" of minority workers. Failure to comply could lead to exclusion from government contracts, fines and backpay awards. Despite legal challenges, by 1972 federal contractors were required to meet goals and timetables regarding affirmative action (Blumrosen, 1994).

---

*Civil Rights Act, 1991*

This Act was introduced to overrule a number of Supreme Court decisions which were seen as weakening enforcement of the laws against employment discrimination (Burstein, 1994: 370). However, the Act also prohibited the practice of "race norming", whereby rankings on tests were calculated separately for different ethnic groups.

*Changes in Interpretation of the Law*

During the Reagan Administration, affirmative actions were challenged through the Justice Department. During the period 1983 to 1989, action by the EEOC was also watered down and it brought no "adverse impact" suits or cases that used statistics to prove purposeful discrimination. The decline in class action, job discrimination lawsuits from 1,174 in 1976 to just 48 in 1987 suggest a significant change in the application of these laws despite the lack of change in the letter of the law.

---

## Box 8.3: EU Equal Pay and Equal Opportunities Policy

---

*Treaty of Rome*

Article 119 expressed "the principle that men and women should receive equal pay for equal work". Pay is defined to include both basic wages and any other cash or non-cash benefits provided by the employer.

*Equal Pay Directive 1975*

Contained the principle of equal pay for work of equal value; however, there has been no litigation in this area in a number of Member States — France, Luxembourg, Greece, and Italy (European Commission, 1994). Implementation of this principle is restricted by the absence of definition or clarification in national legislation (Italy, Belgium, Luxembourg., Spain, Greece and Portugal). The Directive did not specify how equal value should be established and Member States have adopted a variety of different mechanisms: e.g. in Belgium, France, Italy, Luxembourg and Germany, responsibility lies with "work inspectorates" while in the Netherlands equal value is assessed using a job evaluation system.

*Equal Treatment Directive, 1976*

Called for equal treatment for men and women "as regards access to employment, vocational training, promotion and working conditions." It also called for the elimination of indirect sex discrimination.

*Amsterdam Treaty, 1997*

Reaffirms commitment to equality between men and women. A new Article 13 permits appropriate action to combat all forms of discrimination. Article 137 commits the EU to support and complement the activity of Member States in promoting equality between men and women with regard to labour market opportunities and treatment at work. Article 141 extends the scope of the original Article 119, to incorporate developments in EU equality policy. For example, it includes the principle of equal pay for work of equal value, and that of equal opportunities and equal treatment in matters of employment and occupation. It also states that *"the principle of equal treatment shall not prevent any Member State from maintaining or adopting measures providing for specific advantages in order to make it easier for the underrepresented sex to pursue a vocational activity or to prevent or compensate for disadvantages in professional careers."* This allows for the possibility of "affirmative action". The boundaries of such action will be set by the European Courts of Justice. In rulings to date the court has accepted that positive action in favour of women is compatible with European Law except for the specific case of unconditional preferential quotas.

*Employment Guidelines 1999*

Commitments to gender equality are also contained in the Employment Guidelines. The first set of guidelines were adopted by the Commission at the 1997 Jobs Summit. A revised set of guidelines was adopted in 1999 and each Member State is required to produce a National Action Plan to implement them. The guidelines include commitments to take action on reducing gender gaps in employment, unemployment and wages, reducing tax-benefit disincentives, implementing family friendly policies, eliminating obstacles facing returners, and setting in place procedures to monitor progress in these areas. However, the guidelines lack the force of a Directive and the equality guidelines lack any specific targets, therefore their implementation is less than certain.

## 8.4 TRADE UNION POLICIES/COLLECTIVE BARGAINING

Comparative studies are providing a growing body of evidence that centralised wage bargaining is associated with narrower gender wage differentials (Almond and Rubery, 1998; Whitehouse, 1992; Kidd and Shannon, 1996). Centralised wage bargaining is found to compress overall wage inequality, which improves the situation of women and others concentrated in the lower end of the income distribution. Centralised wage agreements also reduce inter-firm differences in wages, which have been found to be an important source of gender differences in earnings (Petersen and Morgan, 1995). Furthermore, the existence of corporatist bargaining structures has been found to facilitate the implementation of legislative initiatives to narrow the gender wage gap (Kidd and Shannon, 1996).

Irish industrial relations have passed through a number of phases regarding collective wage agreements.[6] The State first intervened in the wage bargaining process during the 1970s by setting up a series of National Wage Agreements. A number of these agreements incorporated differential levels of pay for men and women and so solidified rather than reduced gender wage differences. The agreements were not properly enforced and second-tier bargaining became the norm. The strategy collapsed in 1981 and was replaced by decentralised wage bargaining for a six-year period from 1981–1987. This period saw increased wage differentials and a deterioration of the position of the low paid because they were no longer protected by the minimum wage increases in the national wage agreements. Centralised wage bargaining was reintroduced under the under the first Partnership Agreement, the Programme for National Recovery (1987–1990) and persists up to the current programme — the Programme for Prosperity and Fairness.

Analysis of trends in wages in private sector employment in four sectors of the economy between 1987 and 1993 showed that the first two partnership agreements "imposed a significant degree of uniformity on private sector wage movements" (Sexton and O'Connell, 1996: 60). However, this did not prevent an in-

---

[6] This section draws on Chapters 4 and 5 of Sexton and O'Connell (eds.), 1996.

crease in wage inequality over the same time period (Barrett et al., 1999; and Chapter 4 above). Given the international evidence of the effect of centralised wage bargaining on wage inequality, it is possible that the rise in inequality would have been even larger in the absence of the Partnership Agreements. Under the conditions of the agreements, wages in the public sector increased at a slightly higher rate (4.5 per cent). Given women's over-representation in the public sector, this trend may have contributed to the narrowing of the total wage gap observed in the empirical analyses.

However, there are a number of limitations to advancing gender pay equality through trade unions and collective bargaining. The key to benefiting from such collective wage agreements is representation. The rate of union membership in Ireland has declined throughout the 1980s from a peak of 62 per cent in 1980 (Roche, 1994). Evidence from the 1997 Labour Force Survey suggests that only 44 per cent of employees are members of trade unions or staff associations: 45 per cent of male employees and 43 per cent of female employees. Membership was adversely affected by the high rates of unemployment and the influx of multinational companies who have resisted union recognition. High levels of unionisation in the Irish public sector (77 per cent) have prevented further decline in union density and have prevented a wider gap in male and female union participation.[7]

Membership alone does not ensure equal representation. The organisational structures of the unions have been male-dominated and this has discouraged activism amongst women. Despite recent efforts to redress the balance, women continue to be under-represented among full-time union officials and on TU decision-making bodies (ICTU, 1998). British studies have shown that, historically, trade unions have played a major role upholding gender differences through exclusionary practices and down-playing of women's skills (Walby, 1986; Rubery, 1980). In the past, Irish unions signed up to wage agreements that institutionalised sex differences in pay (see footnote 3 above) and supported the marriage bar (Cousins, 1996). O'Connor (1998) argues that, up to the late 1980s, Irish unions were "mainly concerned with the

---

[7] Union membership figures come from author's own analysis of the 1997 LFS.

creation of full-time male jobs in manufacturing industries". Since the introduction of equality legislation, some unions have been active in taking equal pay claims; ICTU (1993) report that between 1987 and 1992, nine trade unions took a total of 90 equal pay cases under the Anti-Discrimination (Pay) Act. However, it remains important for trade unions to monitor how effectively they are representing the interests of women.

For the majority of workers who are not represented by trade unions, the collective agreements will provide no protection unless their employer is a member of a participating employers' organisation. The last two partnership agreements have attempted to broaden consultation by including representation from women's groups, the unemployed and other voluntary groups; however, their involvement in wage negotiations is likely to be limited.

## 8.5 THE MINIMUM WAGE AND WAGE INEQUALITY

Another policy which may reduce both wage dispersion and the gender wage gap is the national minimum wage (NMW). A National Minimum Wage of £4.40 per hour was introduced in April 2000. Analysis presented in Chapter 6 and research conducted by Nolan and McCormick (1999) has shown that women would benefit disproportionately from the introduction of a minimum wage. Nolan and McCormick (1999) estimated that 55 per cent of those affected by a minimum wage of £4.40 would be women. This result arises from the fact that 17 per cent of women employees are calculated to fall below the minimum wage level, compared to 11 per cent of male employees. Part-timers are particularly over-represented among the low-paid and therefore constitute a high proportion of those who would benefit from a minimum wage (approximately one-third).[8] The analysis in Chapter 6 above showed that the effect of the NMW on gender differentials depends on the value of the minimum wage, but that at the level

---

[8] The over-representation of women and part-timers among those affected by a minimum wage is consistent with results from the UK (Low Pay Commission, 1998).

proposed, a rise in the female-to-male wage ratio of under 1 percentage point might be expected.

The extent to which a minimum wage would lead to an overall narrowing of the wage distribution depends in part on whether those above the minimum attempt to reassert wage differentials. This is known as the "spill-over" effect. Evidence from other countries suggest that spill-over effects are confined to the bottom end of the wage distribution and to those working closely with employees on the minimum wage, and that the net result is still a substantial narrowing of wage differences (Nolan and McCormick, 1999: 66).

While the introduction of the minimum wage is likely to have a positive effect on female-to-male wage ratios, it is a limited one. A further consideration is the future evolution of the level of the minimum wage. Almond and Rubery (1998) warn that if governments keep the level of the minimum wage low as a means of encouraging wage restraint higher up the wage distribution, the outcome is likely to be more gender inequality rather than less. They therefore argue that minimum wage levels should be gender-audited. This is consistent with the policy proposed by the Commission on the Status of Women.

## 8.6 STRATEGIES TO REDUCE THE IMPACT OF CAREER INTERRUPTIONS

The analysis in Chapter 3 showed that a very large part of the "explained" variance in the gender wage gap was due to differences in accumulated work experience and years spent outside the labour market. Longitudinal studies of individuals' careers have also demonstrated that when women return to work from a period of full-time childcare they often experience occupational downgrading, reduced earnings and fewer promotion opportunities (McRae, 1993; Joshi and Hinde, 1993). This downward mobility following career interruptions may also be partially responsible for the lower returns to education found for women in the earlier analysis. Therefore, it appears that policies aimed at shortening the period spent outside the labour market, or for re-integrating female workers who have taken career breaks, are essential if gaps between men's and women's average wages are to be reduced.

## Childcare

It is widely believed that substantial improvement in childcare provision is a *sine qua non* if the long-term labour market attachment of women is to be increased. The provision of good quality, affordable childcare services would, it is argued, reduce the necessity to take time out of employment and allow mothers to compete in the labour market on more equal terms. This is not to say that, even with such childcare services in place, differences in men's and women's labour market participation (and associated wage gaps) would be likely to disappear.[9] We consider first the statistical profile of the usage of paid childcare as of 1997; move on to examine more recent developments in childcare policy; and then explore some key issues for future policy in this area.

### Statistical Profile of Usage of Paid Childcare

Figures on childcare are not routinely collected in Ireland. In a special survey of parents' childcare arrangements undertaken by the ESRI for the Commission on the Family, it was found that the majority of mothers in paid employment used informal types of childcare (Williams and Collins, 1998). For example, among mothers of children aged 0 to 4, engaged in full-time paid work, 56 per cent used childminders, 8 per cent used paid relatives and a further 22 per cent used unpaid forms of care. Only 14 per cent relied fully on crèches, nurseries, kindergartens or other forms of pre-school (Fahey, 1998). Even among the minority "formal childcare" category, very few places were publicly funded. Goodbody et al. (1999) estimated that some £20 million of State and EU funds were being spent annually on childcare provision in 1998/9, largely targeted at children in need or in disadvantaged circumstances. This compares with private expenditure on childcare (estimated from the special ESRI survey referred to above) of about £170 million. Thus, state funding of childcare stood at about 10 per cent of

---

[9] See, for example, Jenkins and Symons (1995), an econometric study which finds that while childcare costs do have the expected disincentive effects on the labour market participation of lone mothers, the effects were not as great as expected.

total expenditure on childcare at that time.[10] In part as a result of the relatively low level of state subsidy (via price subsidies, benefits or tax reliefs) the cost of childcare as a proportion of average earnings in Ireland is amongst the highest in the EU (Expert Working Group on Childcare, 1999).

State-aided childcare has been very much focused on disadvantaged or at-risk children. Most children and most parents with childcare needs have not been the targets of state-aided childcare until quite recently.[11] The Expert Working Group on Childcare (1999: *xxi*) note that while demand for childcare is increasing, the number of places is dropping because of staff shortages and the fact that some existing childcare facilities have been unable to meet the requirements of recently introduced regulations.

*National Childcare Strategy, National Development Plan and Budget 2000*

The *National Childcare Strategy* (developed by an Expert Working Group under Partnership 2000) made a number of recommendations to improve the supply of and support the demand for childcare. The measures suggested include providing capital and employment grants, tax relief and other forms of funding for those supplying childcare. The *Strategy* also recommended a special tax allowance for childminding earnings, and that such income should be disregarded for a number of benefits, including medical cards, in order to encourage childminders to enter the formal economy where standards can be regulated.

To help parents with the costs of childcare, the Working Group recommended tax relief of up to £4,000 for each child un-

---

[10] The Programme for Economic and Social Progress incorporated incentives to employers to provide childcare facilities at the workplace. The scheme appears to have had a low take-up and the Working Group on Childcare Facilities (1994: 25) highlights a number of limitations of workplace nurseries including fluctuations in demand due to age structure of employees; the expense involved for small or medium-sized firms; lack of space; and potentially unsuitable environments for children.

[11] The State also subsidises the provision of childcare through public sector workplace nurseries, for example those operating in Third Level Institutes, the Civil Service, the IDA, etc. (Working Group on Childcare Facilities for Working Parents, 1994). Again, the numbers catered for in these nurseries is small as a proportion of the eligible age group.

der 12, at the standard tax rate only. For those with low or zero tax liabilities, a number of targeted measures were recommended (direct subsidies for those in education or training, increases in FIS income limits, and an increase in the earnings ceiling for One Parent Family benefit). It was recommended that tax relief or subsidies be conditional on formally receipted payment for care, so that the quality of care being paid for can be monitored and evaluated. The rationale for this overall approach was that resources would be targeted directly at those who need to purchase childcare, and that it would encourage the formalisation and regulation of the childcare sector.

The National Development Plan (1999) provided for an overall envelope of £250 million for expenditure on childcare over a six-year period. The objectives stated included childcare for the purpose of making education, training and labour market opportunities more accessible, particularly to women in disadvantaged communities and to single-parent families. But the Plan has an equal opportunities as well as a social inclusion focus: "It will [also] address the needs of men and women generally in reconciling their childcare needs with their participation in the labour force."

While the Plan gives a broad indication of priorities and the overall resource envelope, the first indication of how the resources will actually be employed came in Budget 2000. On expenditures exclusively associated with childcare, the main priority was given to increasing the supply of childcare places, and measures to improve the quality of childcare. Total funding earmarked for childcare came to £45 million in a full year. About half of this was allocated to expansion of the Equal Opportunities Childcare Programme of the Department of Justice, Equality and Law Reform: this programme has, since 1998, had both a social inclusion and equal opportunities perspective.[12] On the demand side, Child Benefit was increased by £1.84 per week; a relatively

---

[12] Other major expenditures included £10 million for a grant scheme for small-scale childcare providers towards the capital costs of upgrading their premises, often a requirement of the recently introduced Childcare (Pre-School Services) Regulations. A further £5 million each was provided for schools which set up and run after-school childcare services, and for community groups developing out-of-school hours services.

small contribution in the context of total childcare costs. The concentration of tax relief on single people and two-earner couples will also have helped to boost the incomes of many families with high childcare costs, though this measure is principally aimed at a different goal: reducing the number of taxpayers facing the top rate of tax.

*Some Strategic Issues*

The issues associated with changes in the level and structure of state support for childcare are many and complex. While in the context of this report, the main focus is on an equal opportunities perspective, we must broaden our focus in order to consider how best the state may structure financial support for childcare in future. The "how" of childcare support depends intimately on the "why". The reasons for an increase in state financial support for childcare are discussed in some depth in Callan and Farrell (1991). To summarise, the most compelling arguments for state support are those which relate to:

- The early education benefits of a stimulating environment for children (which is not to say that this cannot be provided by parents within the home);

- The equalisation of opportunities between the sexes; and

- The provision of special support to disadvantaged families.

At the outset we should make clear that there is a strong case for a particular focus on disadvantage, with extra resources going to this group. In recent years, there has been a move away from an exclusive focus on disadvantage towards a policy motivated also by concern about equal opportunities. However, there remains, and is likely to remain, a large gap between the level of subsidy for disadvantaged groups and for those benefiting from state childcare subsidies on a more general basis. It is on how this general level of support is to be set and structured that we mainly focus here.

In our view the appropriate general level and structure of childcare support is inextricably linked with restructuring the level and nature of income support for children more generally.

Any attempt to "solve" the childcare issue independently of broader child income support will, in our view, lead to a less than optimal outcome from a societal point of view.[13] Turning to the Irish case, in thinking about the level of state financial support for the care of young children, it is of some interest to compare the levels of public investment in children of different ages. It is important to recognise that a major element of that support is the provision of free education (on a compulsory basis for those aged 6 to 15). While Child Benefit remains at the same rate for children of all ages, it is dwarfed by the cost of the subsidy to education at different levels. Even at primary level, where the subsidy is lowest, it is of the order of £1,000 per pupil per year. This lacuna in the state's investment strategy was recognised by the Commission on the Family.[14] The care of young children, apart from some support in terms of physical health care, has been treated as essentially a private matter until recently. But many of the reasons for free, compulsory primary education are also relevant to younger age groups.

While the issues are complex, a simple approach helps to illustrate a fundamental and, as yet, unanswered question regarding the foundations of a rational policy. Government policy, as derived from manifesto commitments in the last general election, recognised the following as desiderata:

A.  Additional financial support for paid childcare; and

B.  Additional financial support for childcare undertaken by parents in the home.

---

[13] Countries can be seen as occupying different positions on a spectrum ranging from little state intervention and support to very extensive intervention and support. Ireland, along with the UK, are at the low levels of intervention and support end of this spectrum. The US, often seen as the bastion of nonintervention, has a tax-based support structure. Scandinavian countries and France tend to have high levels of intervention and support including publicly provided and funded facilities. Country positions on this spectrum reflect a range of influences from historical accident to deeply held values and attitudes expressed through the political system.

[14] "Apart from child benefit and limited intervention programmes for some children at risk of educational or social disadvantage, there is almost no state investment in the care of children in the years before entry into primary school."

A key question in this regard is whether the level of additional support is to be the *same* for purchasers of paid childcare (often two-earner couples or lone parents) and providers of "own account" childcare; or whether one or other group is to receive a higher subsidy. Research can illuminate the economic and social implications of either decision, but ultimately the choice is one for society at large, operating through the political system.

- If (A) were to receive a higher level of additional support than (B), then the likelihood is that women's labour market attachment would increase, and in the long term the wage gap would be reduced. If, on the other hand, (B) were to receive greater additional support than (A), then the likelihood is that labour market attachment would be reduced and the wage gap would tend to increase in the long-term.

- If either (A) or (B) is to receive a higher level of support, then two types of payment or financial support would be required. But if the additional financial support is to have the same value for those using purchased childcare and those caring directly for their own children, then a single payment mechanism is preferable.

- "Labelled" payments for each group may be seen as politically more acceptable, but are liable to leave unintended gaps in coverage and may lead to some distortion of choices regarding modes of childcare.

- The criticism that increases in Child Benefit are "not enough" usually carries with it the implication that income support for some children or some families should be greater than for others.

- A child benefit type mechanism (with payments related to the age of the children) has much to recommend it. Refundable tax credits would achieve much the same end, but require the design of a new and more complex delivery mechanism. On the other hand, there are some potential advantages to refundable tax credits. Refundable tax credits could achieve the same end-result as a child benefit increase in terms of household incomes, while staying within the government's target on limitation of government expenditure. More importantly, the use of the refundable tax credit mechanism could help to heal the rift between those regarding themselves as "taxpayers", who may tend to discount rather heavily payments received through child benefit, and those regarding themselves as "welfare recipients", for whom tax breaks are irrelevant.

- One theme running through the report of the Expert Working Group (*National Childcare Strategy*) was a concern that demand-side supports would simply lead to a rise in the price of childcare, with little increase in supply in the short run. While it is true that attention to the supply-side is needed in the short run, this should not preclude a rise in prices. Significant increases in childcare prices are needed to raise wages and profits in the sector — the signal which will attract more resources into that sector. Thus, demand-side supports should not be rejected on the grounds that they will raise prices: this is a necessary part of a long-run solution. There is, of course, also a need to boost the supply side, particularly in upgrading or providing premises to meet the new childcare regulations.

- Another theme in the policy debate is a concern to ensure that the benefits of childcare subsidies do not flow towards childcare providers (often thought to include many in the childminding sector) who are not fully compliant with the tax and welfare regulations. A related concern is that childcare providers should be included in the tax and welfare system. Some of the policies proposed with these concerns in mind carry the danger that a two-speed system might emerge, with high quality and officially subsidised services, used mainly by those in middle and higher income groups; and unregistered services outside the tax net, used mainly by lower income groups.

We noted earlier that some of the strongest reasons for investing in childcare relate to equality of opportunity, disadvantaged families, and the developmental benefits of high quality childcare. But there is another reason, which is often neglected. Society has an interest in the welfare of all citizens, including the youngest ones. Even if there were no investment-type benefits from high quality childcare, there are certainly consumption benefits for the youngest citizens in having good quality care available not only inside but outside the family home. Improving the quality of life for these younger citizens, just as for adults and the elderly, can be a legitimate social objective. From a free market perspective, one might question why or what sort of government intervention is necessary. To a large extent, the welfare of adults is left to private consumption decisions, once cash resources have been redistributed by the tax and welfare systems. But even for adults, certain goods and services are given a special status ("merit goods") and publicly provided or subsidised. Compulsory education is one of these; but a similar rationale could also apply to childcare.

## Maternity Leave

The extent of maternity leave in Ireland is low compared to other countries in Europe; only Luxembourg grants a shorter total period of statutory maternity leave (European Commission Network on Children, 1996). Female employees are entitled to only 14 weeks' paid maternity leave during which they receive 70 per cent of former earnings (European Commission, 1999). An additional four weeks' unpaid leave can be taken at the employee's request; this also compares unfavourably to the length of extended unpaid or reduced rate leave provided elsewhere in Europe. Longer maternity leave could encourage more women to remain in the labour market, increase job tenures and facilitate greater continuity in women's careers. The Government's *Action Programme for the Millennium* contains a commitment to review and improve existing maternity provision.

## Parental Leave

Flexible parental leave schemes again allow parents to take short periods out of work for family responsibilities and so make longer breaks and employer changes unnecessary. Prior to the introduction of the Parental Leave Act, 1998, Ireland was one of only three countries in the EU without any statutory parental leave (Rubery et al., 1999: 161). The 1998 Act introduced a statutory entitlement for both parents to 14 weeks of unpaid leave. The leave must be taken before the child is five, and is non-transferable between parents. The leave can be taken in a continuous block or, by agreement between employer and employee, as a number of broken periods. The Act also gives all employees limited time off for family emergencies.

The EU Directive on which the Parental Leave Act was based allowed individual member states to decide if the leave was to be paid or unpaid. Seven of the EU15 provide paid parental leave; Ireland, like the UK, the Netherlands and most of the Southern European countries only offer unpaid leave (Rubery et al., 1999).[15] The lack of payment is likely to mean that many families will be unable to afford to avail of this "right". The National Social and Economic Council has expressed concern that because the leave is unpaid, "it will remain an option open only to those on higher incomes" (NESC, 1999: 42). The loss of income might be more sustainable if employers are flexible in how parental leave is taken, for example as a day per week rather than in one block. The Irish scheme is also limited in duration compared to provision in some other EU countries. For example, France, Germany, Finland, Spain and Sweden offer up to three years' leave (European Commission Network on Childcare, 1996).

The Government as employer offers somewhat better leave opportunities for those working in the public sector; for example, the civil service career break scheme allows a period of unpaid leave of between six months and five years for domestic reasons or educational purposes. Re-employment at the same grade following the career break is not necessarily immediate but is guaranteed within 12 months of the finish date. In addition, a pilot scheme of term-time working was introduced in four Government Departments in 1999. This scheme allows parents to take 10 or 13 weeks of leave over the summer to coincide with school holidays. The leave is unpaid but participants can arrange to have their remaining annual salary paid in equal amounts over 12 months. The pilot scheme was only available to full-time employees, which is likely to exclude a category of workers with childcare responsibilities. Employment practice within the civil service and public

---

[15] The countries providing paid leave are Belgium, Denmark, Italy, Austria, Finland, Sweden and France. In France paid leave is only available to families with more than one child.

sector can set an example for other employers; therefore, the State's continued role in formulating and implementing "family-friendly" work practices for its employees is very important. In the current tight labour market, however, private sector employers may show more flexibility than the state as employer.

### Assistance for Women Re-entering the Job Market

Training programmes and job search assistance for women re-entering the workforce would allow better matching and potentially less wage and occupational downgrading for this group. Under the current system of access to training courses, women returners are disadvantaged by rules that give priority to those on the Live Register. Women re-entering the job market are usually ineligible for unemployment benefits and therefore will not appear on the register.[16] FÁS runs a Return to Work programme, which is targeted at those hoping to re-enter the job market and has recently piloted a locally based scheme for women returners, Local Action for Women. However, there is no evidence as to whether these schemes improve women's employment chances and wage levels compared to other women with the same background characteristics who do not enter these programmes. It remains an open question whether returners would be better served by gaining access to all courses on an equal footing with the registered unemployed. Research by O'Connell and McGinnity (1997) shows that women seeking to re-enter the labour market are more likely to participate in less effective programmes.

### Flexible Working Arrangements

The policies for reducing the negative impact of career interruptions have so far focused on strategies to adapt workers' behaviour; the alternative is to adapt the jobs themselves. The most common of these arrangements is part-time working, but other strategies include job-sharing, teleworking, flexitime and working from home. Part-time work is less common in Ireland than the EU

---

[16] Women who have paid PRSI contributions for two full consecutive tax years at any stage in their working life can apply for PRSI credits and so appear on the register in this way. However, this group are given lower priority for access to training/employment schemes than the long-term unemployed.

average; in 1997, 23 per cent of women worked part-time, and three-quarters of all part-timers were female. Job-sharing involves dividing one full-time job into two or more positions but differs from part-time work in that the incumbents are entitled to the same terms and conditions of the full-time job on a pro rata basis. This arrangement is more common in public sector employment. Research carried out in 1994 suggested that 2.2 per cent of private sector employees and approximately 3.3 per cent of public sector employees were job sharers (Fynes et al., 1996). Information on the incidence of other flexible arrangements in Ireland is more limited. A recent study of SMEs (Fisher, 2000) found that 31 per cent of these companies operated flexitime arrangements, and 28 per cent operated teleworking or working from home arrangements. However in the majority of firms these were provided on an informal, case by case basis and it was noted that "the overall number of employees availing of such arrangements is small" (Fisher, 2000). EU data suggest that only 4.4 per cent of the Irish workforce are engaged in teleworking. Current labour shortages are likely to mean that employers are more likely to accommodate demands for flexible hours, so their incidence may have increased.

In Chapter 2, we saw that part-time women earn an average of £6.22 per hour compared to £6.46 for full-timers (Table 2.7). The analysis in Chapter 7 shows that this difference is not due to differential rewards for the same human capital (education and experience) but to differences in the characteristics of full-timers and part-timers, including unobserved characteristics which have an impact on participating full-time and on wages.[17] The Irish results are quite different from those in the US, the UK, Canada and Australia, which show a strong negative impact of part-time work on hourly wages, despite occupational controls (Gornick and Jacobs, 1996).

Although current part-time work was found not to contribute to the overall gender wage gap, the effect of introducing greater work flexibility on gender wage equality remains somewhat am-

---

[17] Analysis of the *Living in Ireland Survey* by O'Connell and Gash (1999) suggests that differences in occupational location can also explain the relatively small gap in the wages of part-time and full-time women.

biguous if these options continue to be taken predominantly by women. The analysis above could not include information on years spent in part-time work and so assess the longer-term impact of part-time working on the gender wage gap — research in the US suggests that years of part-time work explain a significant proportion of sex differences in wages.[18] There is also qualitative evidence that flexible working can damage women's promotion prospects. For example, in a study of Irish Health Boards, O'Connor (1995) found that when women availed of job-sharing or career breaks, this was seen to indicate lower levels of commitment and thereby reduced women's promotion possibilities. Part-timers have also been found to lose out in terms of non-wage compensation, such as pensions, health insurance, etc. (Dex, 1992). A further disadvantage is that part-time working among women fails to challenge traditional gender roles within the household (Layte, 1999), which is a major source of female disadvantage in the labour market. Therefore, if the introduction of flexible work options is to reduce the gender wage gap, it needs to be accompanied by changes in organisational culture, so that employment commitment is not equated with long hours, and by changes in attitudes so that options to combine work and family life are taken up by both men and women.

## 8.7 STRATEGIES TO REDUCE GENDER SEGREGATION IN THE LABOUR MARKET

### Sources of Gender Segregation

Another potential route towards generating greater gender equality in wages is the reduction of gender segregation in the labour market. As argued in Chapter 4 above, comparing the wages of men and women within finer occupational groups is likely to lead to smaller wage gaps but it does not demonstrate the absence of discrimination. Discrimination in recruitment or promotion procedures, sexual harassment, or exclusionary practices by trade unions can lie behind occupational gender segregation,

---

[18] Corcoran and Duncan (1979) found that the proportion of working years spent in full-time work accounted for 8 per cent of the wage gap, compared to 6 per cent explained by years out of the labour force.

as can unequal access to education or training schemes. Gender segregation in the labour market can also result from non-discriminatory processes such as differences in men's and women's educational and career aspirations — in which case, anti-discrimination and equal opportunity policies might have quite limited impact on the degree of segregation. The view that occupational segregation is largely a consequence of women's supply-side decisions has received some attention in the recent sociological literature through the work of Hakim (1996a, 1996b, 1993, 1992). Hakim argues that gender segregation and wage gaps persist because a significant proportion of working women are secondary earners who are not committed to employment, work part-time and/or intermittently, value convenience factors above pay, and do not seek training or advancement. These secondary earners are believed to prefer to work in female-dominated occupations which facilitate part-time working and breaks in employment (1996a: 207). From this point of view, segregation is not a matter for policy concern because for this group it is a result of individual choice.[19]

Hakim's thesis has been widely criticised for failing to take account of the structural conditions within which women make decisions about paid work (e.g. the availability of childcare, structure of job opportunities, maternity provision, social insurance and benefit rules, etc.), and for assuming that women's orientations to work are stable across their lifetime (O'Reilly and Fagan, 1998; Ginn et al., 1996). There is also little evidence that female-dominated occupations are less punishing of career breaks or that women with continuous labour force participation are less likely to be in predominantly female occupations (see Marini (1989) for a review). Furthermore there is no *a priori* reason why some high-skilled jobs cannot be organised on a part-time basis.

### Irish Evidence
While the causes of segregation are debated, there is no dispute that the Irish labour market continues to be highly segregated by sex (see Chapter 4). Recent work by Ruane and Sutherland (1999:

---

[19] Similar arguments are made in the economic literature by Polachek (1981).

47) shows high levels of segregation by industrial sector; in 1997 women represented 38 per cent of all workers but comprised 80 per cent of service sector workers, 9 per cent of agricultural sector workers and 24 per cent of industrial sector workers. Men and women are also highly segregated in occupational terms. In 1997, over 67 per cent of females were employed in just three occupations: clerical workers, professional and technical workers and service workers (ibid.: 51). As shown in Chapter 2, however, the concentration of women in these three sectors did not contribute greatly to an explanation of the overall wage gap. Rather, it was differences between men and women within these broad occupational groupings which contributed most to the explanation of the overall wage gap.

Within the broad occupational groupings, there is considerable evidence that women tend to cluster at lower levels of the occupational hierarchy. This phenomenon is known as vertical gender segregation. The third-level educational sector provides a clear example of vertical gender segregation: only 3 per cent of professors/associate professors and 9 per cent of senior lecturers are female, while in the lowest rank of junior lecturer, 52 per cent are women (Ruane and Sutherland, 1999: 70). Another indicator of the "glass ceiling" is the figure that less than 3 per cent of the top executives in Ireland are female (ibid: 69).

It is clear that vertical segregation is linked very directly to the gender wage gap. The evidence on whether horizontal segregation contributes to the wage gap is less clear-cut. Horizontal segregation by occupation and sector could be important for the gender wage gap because occupations are valued differently and paid differently. It can be argued that differences in pay between occupations arise not only from differences in the productivity and skills of the workers or in the demands of the job, but also from market position, the relative bargaining strengths of different groups and traditional patterns of pay differences between jobs. Low levels of pay and status in some jobs occupied predominantly by women can in part be attributed to women's lack of bargaining power in the process of skill definition (see the discussion of women and trade unions above).[20] Market forces can, however, play a role in eliminating any such undervaluation, as reductions in the supply of new entrants to such occupations (or exits to other sectors, as has happened in the case of nursing in recent years) can lead to upward wage pressure.

While the occupational groupings used in Chapter 2 were very broad, a more detailed analysis confirms the picture obtained there.[21] Occupations were divided into 21 categories, as in the Labour Force Survey, and average male and female wages calculated for each of these categories. If women's wages were equal to men's wages within each of these categories, the average woman's wage would be higher than the average male wage. This arises because women tend to be concentrated in sectors which are higher paid, when ranked by *male* wages. If, on the other hand, women were distributed across the 21 occupations in the same proportions as men, but continued to receive the average female wage within each occupation, the wage ratio would be virtually unchanged. While this analysis is a limited one, it does point to vertical rather than horizontal segregation as the major source of wage differences.

Policies dealing directly with skill and job evaluations were considered in Section 8.3. In what follows we look at different strategies for reducing both vertical and horizontal gender segregation within employment.

### Education System

The education system is an early source of gender differences, which can later result in labour market segregation. The influence of schooling on gender segregation can arise from both formal and informal processes. At a formal level, the availability and timetabling of subjects can have important gender consequences.

---

[20] A number of researchers have also noted that jobs that involve caring skills or other "domestic" skills such as nursing or childminding have been under-valued because they are seen to rely on some natural feminine ability rather than skill (Jenson, 1989; Walby, 1986).

[21] The analysis is not reported here in detail as in some instances the numbers of cases on which average wages are calculated is rather small; but similar results are obtained when attention is restricted to occupations represented by 25 or more men or women.

In recent years, girls have been outperforming boys at Junior and Leaving Certificate levels (Hannan et al., 1996). Of itself, this might suggest that female labour market entrants could command a higher wage than their male counterparts. But significant differences in subject choices at both second and third level may exert a countervailing influence (Department of Education and Science, 1998; Clancy, 1995). For example, at third level, females constituted about half (49 per cent) of all entrants, but represented a large majority of those going into Education (81 per cent) and Hotel, Catering and Tourism (73 per cent), and formed only 17 per cent of entrants into Technology (Clancy, 1995). These differences in subject area may well contribute to the differential returns to education found for men and women in the earlier models.

The Department of Education and Science has initiated a number of schemes and research projects to promote non-traditional subject choices. For example, research is underway on the topics of "Gender Equality and Mathematics" and "Gender and Science". FUTURES, a curriculum project on stereotyping in subject choice, has been mainstreamed in secondary schools, while NOW projects in the Institutes of Technology provide taster courses in technology subjects for Transition Year girls. Nevertheless, it appears that girls still do not have equal access to technology subjects: girls' schools represent only 2 per cent of schools providing technical graphics, 16 per cent of schools providing Technology, and 22 per cent of the schools providing Computer Studies (Monitoring Committee, 1999: 157–8).

The education system can also influence future gender segregation in a more informal way. The school plays a formative role in socialising young people, building self-confidence and shaping children's aspirations for the future. The importance of this process has been highlighted by research in the US, which show that 61 per cent of young people (aged 14–22) would have to change their occupational aspirations to equalise the distributions of aspirations of the two sexes (Marini and Brinton, 1984). It is therefore important that schools not only offer non-traditional subjects to their pupils but encourage members of both sexes to consider a wide range of educational and career options. It is particularly important that girls are trained in new technologies so that the associated occupations do not become sex-typed.[22]

## Training Options

Equal access to training programmes is another essential step in reducing occupational segregation. Significantly, the Employment Equality Act, 1998, allows for positive action to remove existing inequalities in access to employment, vocational training and promotion. In recent years, FÁS has targeted places on non-traditional and new-technology courses for women and placements have exceeded the target (Monitoring Committee, 1999: 174). However, the number of targeted places was reduced in 1998 and women continue to be under-represented in traditionally male training schemes. This gender divide is particularly noticeable in the apprenticeship system, where women represent less than 1 per cent of trainees (ibid.: 186). This gender gap has persisted despite changing course names and running pre-apprenticeship courses (ESF, 1999). Revision of the content of apprenticeships may be needed to break down this gender division. Greater progression through schemes might also encourage women to take up non-traditional training places.

Both the Commission on the Status of Women and those involved in the EU New Opportunities for Women (NOW) initiatives (1998) have argued that flexible hours on training courses and provision of childcare supports for trainees are essential if women with young children are to gain real access to training opportunities. FÁS considers the Commission's recommendation of direct provision of childcare to be unsustainable (Monitoring Committee, 1999), although this is available on a limited number of Community Employment Schemes. Currently there are no additional childcare allowances for trainees with young children. The experience of the NOW projects also led to recommendations for greater access to information and advice about training opportunities, revision of eligibility requirements to include women

---

[22] Greater opportunities for education will not only decrease segregation but may also effect the gender wage differentials by increasing female participation because women with higher educational qualifications are more likely to remain in the labour market when they have children (see Chapter 7).

returnees and wives of unemployed men, the development of integrated, locally based training and of progression routes from community-based training to mainstream training (1998).

Access to job-related training for those already in the workforce is also likely to influence gender equality in the labour market. Research by O'Connell (1999) shows that in Ireland, a higher proportion of female than male employees participated in job-related training.[23] However, women were less likely to receive employer funding for their training: 34 per cent of the women in job related training were self-funded and 59 per cent were employer-funded, whereas 71 per cent of the men received employer funding and only 15 per cent were self-financed; the proportion receiving government funding was the same for men and women (ibid.: 26). There is a need for further information on the type or quality of job-related training that male and female employees are engaged in and the returns to job-related training by sex in order to examine whether women are making any wage gains for this greater investment in job training.

## Recruitment Procedures

The recruitment process is another obvious target for reducing gender segregation in the labour market. Research has shown that the use of informal recruitment practices — for example, recruiting new employees through the networks of existing employees — is found to reproduce segregated workforces, whether in terms of gender, race or religion (Collinson et al., 1990). Therefore, employment equality agencies discourage the use of such practices and recommend the wide dissemination of job information so that it is accessible to all groups (Employment Equality Agency, 1998). Formalisation is also recommended in the interview process — for example, in the establishment of explicit job requirements and evaluation criteria. The more subjective and informal recruitment criteria are, the more likely the process is to favour men (Goss and Browne, 1991). Greater representation of women on interview boards is also advised (EEA, 1998: 17). While it is recognised that formalising recruitment practices involves some cost (for example,

---

[23] The information was collected in the International Adult Literacy Survey, and related to the year 1994–1995. The figures apply to adults aged 25–64.

the cost of placing advertisements), it does not imply the introduction of elaborate bureaucratic structures; moreover, attracting a diverse group of applicants who fulfil explicit job criteria may have an economic dividend.

## Promotion Practices

Patterns of promotion are important for vertical gender segregation in the labour market and attendant differences in wages. O'Connor (1996) identified a number of important barriers within organisational cultures that prevented women obtaining promotion, which included lack of communication about opportunities, stereotypical attitudes about women's abilities and career aspirations, exclusion from informal male networks, and the absence of women in senior positions to provide support. Even taking the minimum maternity leave was seen by female respondents as an obstacle to promotion:

> There was also a strong feeling that women were deterred
> from applying for promotion if they had already been on Ma
> ternity Leave — almost as if Maternity Leave was a discre
> tionary award which women should feel grateful for receiving
> (O'Connor, 1996: 223).

These problems are seen to be amenable to equal opportunity initiatives, particularly the setting of targets for female promotion. O'Connor (1998, 1996) also highlights a number of barriers that require more radical changes in organisational structures, such as the low ratio of senior to basic posts in predominantly female areas of employment, the distance of female career structures from centres of control over resources, and a lack of visibility of women's work within organisations.

Women's aspirations and self-confidence can also contribute to gender inequality in promotions. A number of studies have found that women apply less frequently for promotion even if they are eligible (see O'Connor, 1998: 238–9, for a review). The long hours culture among management staff and the perceived loss of flexibility may discourage women with family responsibilities from applying for promotion. For example, within the Civil Service, workers may be required to give up flexible work options such as job sharing if they are promoted. Although the Working Hours Directive does not explicitly exclude management from the 48-hour week, the exception relating to those with discretion over their working hours is most likely to apply to management level staff. Therefore the trend towards "presenteeism" needs to be tackled at an organisational level. Limiting excessive working hours will benefit both male and female workers and is unlikely to harm productivity in the long term. The NOW projects aimed at tackling gender gaps in the workplace have also highlighted the importance of giving women access to management training to encourage them to move up the organisational hierarchy.[24]

## 8.8 CONCLUSIONS

As the incidence of direct discrimination becomes less common, more sophisticated approaches are needed to identify the sources of remaining inequalities in male and female hourly wages, and to identify appropriate policy responses. The main aim of policy in this area is to ensure equality of opportunity between the sexes. As stressed earlier, this does not necessarily imply that complete equality of outcome would occur.

Our analysis has demonstrated that continued attachment to the labour market during the childbearing and child-rearing years would have a potentially major impact on the observed wage gap between men and women. In this respect, childcare policies which favour purchased childcare over "own-provided" childcare may tend to be most effective in narrowing the wage gap. On the other hand, the development of state and private sector policies on extended maternity leave, parental leave, flexible working arrangements and a range of family-friendly work practices would also be needed to encourage long-term labour market attachment. The impact of changes in childcare policy alone could be quite limited.

A wide range of other potential policy actions designed to narrow the gap between men's and women's average wages has been discussed above. These include the legislative framework on equality issues and the mechanisms for enforcing its provisions;

---

[24] Projects aimed at cutting the glass ceiling were initiated in companies such as Aer Lingus, Golden Vale, An Garda Síochana and SIPTU.

the potential impact of the national minimum wage; and strategies for the reduction of gender segregation — particularly vertical gender segregation — in the labour market. Issues arising included policies in education, and state and private sector policies
regarding training, recruitment and promotion.

Efforts to promote equal opportunities for men and women
and to reduce the gender wage gap can set up a virtuous circle.
Women's decisions to leave or stay out of the paid workforce are
affected by the type of job and wages they can hope to achieve.
Improving rewards for women in employment is therefore likely
to lead to greater participation, reducing gender differences in
years of experience and time out of the labour market, which will
have a further positive effect on the gender wage gap. The current
shortage of labour has encouraged both the government and employers' organisations to seek greater female participation in the
labour market. In this labour market context, there may be particular opportunities for women to make progress towards greater
labour market equality.

*Chapter 9*

# Conclusions

## 9.1 MAIN FINDINGS

### Measuring the Wage Gap

In Ireland, regular statistics on a full, economy-wide basis for male and female earnings are simply not available. For this reason, undue reliance is often placed on the regularly published series for hourly earnings of men and women in manufacturing. But more than four out of five women work *outside* the manufacturing sector. For this reason, statistics on hourly earnings in manufacturing, however accurate and interesting in themselves, cannot provide a guide to either the level or the trend in the economy-wide gender wage gap.

For a fuller picture, we must rely on the special surveys undertaken by the ESRI. A baseline picture of economy-wide wage differentials in 1987 was already produced using the Survey of Income Distribution, Poverty and Usage of State Services (Callan and Wren, 1994). The present study aimed to bring that picture up to date using information from the first (1994) wave of the *Living in Ireland Survey*, the Irish element of the European Community Household Panel. It has also proved possible to draw on some more recent information from the 1997 wave of the *Living in Ireland* panel.

The ESRI survey data show that average hourly earnings of women in 1987 were about 80 per cent of those of the average man. By 1994, this ratio had risen to just over 82 per cent, with a further rise to 84.5 per cent by 1997. These ratios are about 13 percentage points higher than the corresponding ratios in manufacturing; men in manufacturing have a wage which is reasonably representative of the wages in the wider economy, but women in manufacturing tend to occupy lower-waged jobs than women outside manufacturing.

A special analysis revealed that men were more likely than women to have jobs that included a range of benefits. The most valuable of these is likely to be a pension. When this is taken into account, the gap between men's and women's overall compensation per working hour is 1 or 2 percentage points wider than when only cash earnings are considered.

## Structure of the Wage Gap

A part of this observed wage gap is simply due to differences in the labour-market-relevant characteristics of men and women in paid employment. For example, we know that wages tend to rise with age and labour market experience. But the average woman worker is younger and less experienced than her male counterpart. Using widely applied statistical techniques, we can decompose the total wage gap into a part which is explained by such differences (e.g. in age, labour market experience or education) and leaving a portion which is unexplained. This analysis shows that about half of the total wage gap in 1987 was explained, mainly by differences in labour market experience. By the 1990s, however, almost three-quarters of the gap was explained by such factors.

The "unexplained" wage gap is sometimes treated as the basis for calculating how much higher the average female wage would be "if a woman were paid like a man". It must be recognised, however, that this may give a false impression of how precisely one can measure labour market discrimination. The figure arrived at may be higher or lower than the actual level of discrimination for a number of reasons. No survey can possibly contain data on all the labour-market-relevant characteristics of each employee; and, on the other hand, women facing discrimination (even if it arises outside the labour market) may rationally choose to spend less time in the labour market, thereby reducing their potential future wage. However, the calculation of the so-called "discrimination index" is a useful summary in making comparisons over time and across countries.

The so-called "discrimination index" stood at about 15 per cent in 1987, i.e. the average woman would have earned about 15 per cent more if her characteristics were rewarded in the same way as men's. By the 1990s, however, the index of "discrimination" had fallen to about 5 per cent. Thus, the modest observed rise in women's wages relative to men's concealed a more significant shift in the earnings structure. The "discrimination index" of 5 per cent compares quite favourably with that in the UK and other EU countries.

Why, if the "discrimination index" was falling by about 10 percentage points, did the observed gender wage gap not fall by the same amount? In part, this reflects changes in labour market structure over the period, with a substantial increase in overall wage inequality. As women have tended to be over-represented among the low paid, the shift in the wage structure towards greater vertical inequality has worked to women's disadvantage. Despite this, women's wages have progressed relative to men's, but this gain has been achieved while women were "swimming against the tide" in terms of the increase in overall wage inequality, over the 1987 to 1994 period.

### Potential Causes of the Gap

What are the causes of the wage gap which cannot be explained on the basis of labour market characteristics measured in the survey? Some would argue that the wage gaps arise because sex discrimination lives on "underground", in an illegal fashion, and that more vigorous enforcement is needed. Others would argue that existing laws are well enforced but that the law is too narrow to cope with more sophisticated forms of sex discrimination. Viewed from another angle, some part of the gap in wages may arise because of a long shadow cast by earlier discrimination, including the marriage bar. Even when such discrimination is removed, it can have long-lived effects: higher levels of management and some entire professions may remain male-dominated. One result may be that girls and younger women do not see female role models in senior positions in certain professions or in higher level management within some organisations. Even in times when the typical male and female roles are changing rapidly, personal and social expectations can be heavily influenced by the long-established norm of husband as breadwinner and wife as house-wife — to such an extent that when women break out of the earlier stereotype, they may find themselves expected simply to add their new role as active participants in the paid labour market on top of the traditional "home-making" role.

The most plausible economic theories of discrimination focus particularly on what is termed "statistical discrimination". If, on average, women are likely to have a shorter job tenure, and if there are additional costs associated with the employment of women (e.g. costs of maternity leave) then a profit-maximising employer may have an incentive to hire or promote a man instead of an equally well-qualified woman. This would be illegal under Irish law. But the nature of this economic incentive means that statistical methods of monitoring or enforcement are required, a point to which we will return in the concluding section.

### Earnings and Labour Market Participation

If the overall pay gap is to be closed, the trend towards women staying attached to the paid labour market during the childbearing and child-rearing years would have to continue. This raises complex economic and social issues, some of which fall outside the scope of the current study; the policy section touches on some of these. Here we are concerned with the factual situation regarding links between labour market participation and pay.

Analysis of the factors influencing labour market participation shows that it is the arrival of children that leads to the crucial differences in participation. For a typical man, the arrival of children has little impact on his labour market participation; but a woman with identical qualifications and experience would typically, under current circumstances, end up with nine years less labour market experience by the age of 47. This has a major effect on the wage that can be commanded in the labour market. The wage paths for the man and woman cannot be brought closely into line without a further increase in labour market attachment of women during the childbearing and child-rearing years.

One way of achieving such an increase in labour market attachment in a "family-friendly" fashion is through part-time
working. A key issue here is whether part-time workers experience a wage penalty because of an imbalance between the supply
of, and demand for, part-time workers. Statistical analysis reveals
no significant evidence of such a penalty in Ireland in 1994.

## 9.2 POLICY CONCLUSIONS

While high-quality, affordable childcare is often seen as a *sine qua
non* for true equality of opportunity, it is true that childcare policy
must be designed with more than this in mind: the interests of
children are central, and policy must be geared to facilitating individual choices either to stay in the paid labour market or to take
time out to care for children (and indeed for other family members). Equality of opportunity, rather than complete equality of
outcome, is the declared aim of government policy. Even with a
fully funded high-quality childcare system, some sex differences
in labour market participation could be expected. But the present
situation is far from that point. The Commission on the Family
has pointed to this lacuna in the state's investment strategy, calling for an increased investment in the care of its youngest citizens.
Whether this care should be provided by parents, or purchased by
them from high-quality providers is, we would contend, essentially a choice best left to the parents. State support should, we
believe, be broadly neutral as between different modes of care:
parents, rather than the state, are best placed to decide what suits
their child and their family.

A wide range of other measures are also relevant to the equalisation of opportunities. Recent legislation on equality, and the
nature of its implementation, will play a significant role; the internal structure of trade unions and the nature of bargaining with
employers and in a social partnership framework will also be important. The introduction of a National Minimum Wage will also
have helped to close the pay gap; particular attention must be
given in future to how this wage is to be uprated. Measures designed to make the workplace more family-friendly will also play
a role: these would include parental leave, maternity leave, and, a
key factor in the current environment, assistance for women re-

entering the job market after a period of full-time work in the home. In addition, measures designed to reduce "vertical gender segregation" would help to reduce the wage gap.

If, on average, women are likely to have a shorter job tenure, and if there are additional costs associated with the employment of women (e.g. costs of maternity leave) then a profit-maximising employer may have an incentive to hire or promote a man instead of an equally well-qualified woman. This would be illegal under Irish law. But the nature of this economic incentive means that statistical methods of monitoring or enforcement are required.

We see a need for regular monitoring at four levels:

- At *national* level, the basic statistical requirement is a large, regular household survey with detailed labour market infor-mation from each adult, including earnings and hours worked. This need can be filled either by a regular cross-section survey with such information (e.g. by adding ques-tions on earnings to the Labour Force Survey) or by an annual panel survey such as *Living in Ireland*.

- At *sectoral* level, it may be possible to gather information in other ways; for example, by having some common reporting requirements, a databank could be built up in the public serv-ice which would enable more intensive monitoring of equality issues in future.

- At *firm* level, the key issues include processes of recruitment and promotion, and how staff are allocated to tasks involving a training component or to training courses. Here again, there is a role for common reporting requirements, but also for equality audits by quality-approved analysts, on the direction of the Equality Authority.

- *Cases* investigated by the Office of Equality Investigations should also be monitored to keep track of trends and problem areas; patterns may arise across cases which can be dealt with more effectively at a higher, policy level, than by "firefighting" the individual cases as they arise.

The economic incentive to discriminate can be seen as similar to the economic incentive to evade taxes: it may, in some circumstances, be cheaper to discriminate (e.g. hire a man rather than a somewhat more qualified woman), just as it is cheaper in cash terms to evade a tax liability. But most taxpayers are compliant. Developing a culture of compliance may be more effective than a "big brother" approach to monitoring. Equality audits can act both as a "stick" (somewhat like a tax audit) but also have a more positive function in helping employers to understand and deal with hidden sources of discrimination. It is important that compliance costs should be kept to a reasonable level, in order to avoid unnecessarily raising the costs of employment.

In terms of progress to date, the results suggest that the degree of discrimination in the Irish labour market has fallen between 1987 and 1994. On average, women's hourly wages are now about 85 per cent of the average male wage. About three-quarters of the gap between men's and women's hourly wages can be attributed to the fact that women, under current social and economic structures, typically spend less time in the labour market than men and more time as carers in the home. Unless men and women were to become much more similar in this respect — and views will differ on whether or not this should happen — then complete equality of labour market outcome is not the appropriate yardstick for a policy aiming at equality of opportunity.

# References

Alessio, J.C. and J. Andrexejewski (2000), "Unveiling the Hidden Glass Ceiling: An Analysis of the Cohort Effect Claim", *American Sociological Review*, Vol. 65, pp. 311–315.

Almond, P. and J. Rubery (1998), "The Gender Impact of Recent European Trends in Wage Determination", *Work, Employment and Society*, Vol. 12, No. 4, pp. 675–693.

Baradasi, E. and J.C. Gornick (2000), "Women and Part-time Employment: Workers' 'Choices' and Wage Penalties in Five Industrialised Countries", Institute for Social and Economic Research Working Paper No. 11, University of Essex.

Barrett, A., T. Callan and B. Nolan (1999), "Rising Wage Inequality, Returns to Education and Labour Market Institutions: Evidence from Ireland", *British Journal of Industrial Relations*, Vol. 37, No. 1, pp. 77–100.

Barry, U. and P. Jackson (1988), "Women on the Edge of Time: Part-time Work in Ireland, North and South," in *Women, Equality and Europe*, M. Buckley and M. Anderson (eds.), London: Macmillan.

Barry, U. (2000), "Building the Picture: The Role of Data in Achieving Equality", Opinion Series, Women's Education Research and Resource Centre, University College Dublin, The Equality Authority.

Becker, G. (1957), *The Economics of Discrimination* (2nd Edition, 1971), Chicago: University of Chicago Press.

Benassi, M. (1999), "Women's Earnings in the EU 28 per cent less than Men's", *Statistics in Focus: Population and Social Conditions*, Theme 3-6/1999, Luxembourg: Eurostat.

Bergmann, B. (1999), "The Continuing Need for Affirmative Action", *The Quarterly Review of Economics and Finance*, Vol. 39, pp. 757–768.

Blackwell, J. (1986), *Women in the Labour Force*, Dublin: Employment Equality Agency.

Blackwell, J. (1989), Chapter 4 in *Women in the Labour Force*, Employment Equality Agency and Resource and Environmental Policy Centre, UCD.

Blau, F. and L. Kahn (1991), *The Economics of Childcare*, New York: Russell Sage.

Blau, F. and L. Kahn (1992), "The Gender Earnings Gap: Learning from International Comparisons", *American Economic Review*, Vol. 82, No. 2, pp. 533–38.

Blau, F. and L. Kahn (1994), "Rising Wage Inequality and the US Gender Gap", *American Economic Review*, Vol. 84, No. 2, pp. 23–28.

Blau, F.D. and L.M. Kahn (1999), "Analysing the Gender Pay Gap", *The Quarterly Review of Economics and Finance*, Vol. 39, pp. 625–646.

Blumrosen, A.W. (1994), "The Law Transmission System and the Southern Jurisprudence of Employment Discrimination" in Burstein (ed.) *Equal Employment Opportunity: Labor Market Discrimination and Public Policy*, New York: Aldine de Gruyter.

Blundell, R. (1992), "Labour Supply and Taxation: A Survey", *Fiscal Studies*, Vol. 13, 15–40.

Booth, A., M. Francesconi and J. Frank (1998), "Glass Ceilings or Sticky Floors?", *Centre for Economic Policy Discussion Paper*, No. 1965.

Borjas, G. (1996), *Labour Economics*, New York: McGraw-Hill.

Boyle, G., J. FitzGerald, I. Kearney and D. Smyth (1999), "The Macroeconomic Effects of the Minimum Wage", in B. Nolan (ed.) *The Impact of the Minimum Wage in Ireland*, Appendix B of the *Final Report of the Inter-Departmental Group on Implementation of a National Minimum Wage*, Dublin: Stationery Office.

Burstein, P. (1994) *Equal Employment Opportunity: Labor Market Discrimination and Public Policy*, New York: Aldine de Gruyter.

Cain, G. (1966), *Married Women in the Labour Force: An Economic Analysis*, Chicago: University of Chicago Press.

Callan, T. (1991), "Male–Female Wage Differentials in Ireland", *Economic and Social Review*, Vol. 23, No. 1.

Callan, T., B. Nolan et al. (1989), *Poverty, Income and Welfare in Ireland*, General Research Series, No. 146, Dublin: ESRI.

Callan, T. and B. Farrell (1991), *Women's Participation in the Irish Labour Market*, NESC Report No. 91, Dublin: NESC.

Callan, T. and A. Wren (1994), *Male–Female Wage Differentials: Analysis and Policy Issues*, General Research Series, Paper No. 163, Dublin: ESRI.

Callan, T., S. Adams, S. Dex, S. Gustafsson, J. Schupp and N. Smith (1995), "Gender Wage Differentials: New Cross-country Evidence", ESRI Working Paper 62.

Callan, T. and A. van Soest (1996), *Family Labour Supply and Taxes in Ireland*, ESRI Working Paper 78, Dublin: ESRI.

Callan, T. (1997), *Income Supports and Work Incentives: Ireland and UK*, Dublin: ESRI Policy Research Series.

Card, D. and A. Krueger (1995), *Myth and Measurement*, Princeton University Press.

Central Statistics Office (1997), *Labour Force Survey*, Dublin: Stationery Office.

Clancy, P. (1995), *Access to College:: Patterns of Continuity and Change*, Dublin: Higher Education Authority.

Combat Poverty Agency (2000), *A Better Future for Children: Eliminating Poverty, Promoting Equality*, Combat Poverty Agency.

Collinson, D. (1988), *Barriers to Fair Selection*, Equal Opportunities Commission Research Series, London.

Collinson, D., D. Knights and M. Collinson (1990), *Managing to Discriminate*, London: Routledge.

Cooke, K. (1987), "The Withdrawal from Paid Work of the Wives of Unemployed Men: A Review of Research", *Journal of Social Policy*, Vol. 16, pp. 371–382

Corcoran, M. and G. Duncan (1979), "Work History, Labour Force Attachment and Earnings Differences Between the Races and the Sexes", *Journal of Human Resources*, Vol. 14, No. 1, pp. 3–20.

Cousins, M. (1996), *Pathways to Employment for Women Returning to Paid Work*, Dublin: EEA.

Curtin, D. (1989), *Irish Employment Equality Law*, Dublin: Round Hall Press.

Davies, R., P. Elias and R. Penn (1992), "The Relationship between a Husband's Unemployment and his Wife's Participation", *Oxford Bulletin of Economics and Statistics*, Vol. 54, No. 2, pp. 145–171.

Deere, D., K. Murphy and F. Welch (1996), "Employment and the 1990–91 Minimum Wage Hike", *American Economic Review Papers and Proceedings*, Vol. 85, No. 2, pp. 232–237.

Department of Education and Science (1998), *Statistical Report*, Dublin.

Department of Justice, Equality and Law Reform (1998), *Strategy Statement 1998–2000: Community, Security and Equality*, Dublin.

Dex, S. (1992), "Women's Part-time Work in Britain and the United States" in B. Warme et al. (eds.), *Working Part-time: Risks and Opportunities*, New York: Praeger.

Dickens, R., P. Gregg, S. Machin, A. Manning and J. Wadsworth (1993), "Wage Councils: Was There a Case for Abolition", *British Journal of Industrial Relations*, Vol. 31, No. 4, pp. 515–527.

Doris, A. (1998), "Married Women in the Irish Part-time Labour Market", *Economic and Social Review*, Vol. 29, pp. 157–178.

Durkan, J. (1995), *Women in the Labour Force*, Dublin: Employment Equality Agency.

Employment Equality Agency (1998), *Equality at Work: Policies and Action*, Dublin: EEA.

England, P. (1999), "The Case for Comparable Worth", *The Quarterly Review of Economics and Finance*, Vol. 39, pp. 743–755.

ESF (1999), *Evaluation Report: Equal Opportunities and the ESF*, Dublin: European Social Fund Evaluation Unit.

European Commission (1994), "Memorandum on Equal Pay for Work of Equal Value", Luxembourg: Office for Official Publications of the European Communities.

European Commission (1998), *Equal Opportunities for Women and Men in the European Union: Annual Report 1997*, Luxembourg: Office for Official Publications of the European Communities.

European Commission (1999), *Social Protection in the Member States of the European Union: Situation on 1 January 1998 and Evolution*, Luxembourg: Office for Official Publications of the European Communities.

European Commission Network on Children (1996), *A Review of Services for Young Children in the European Union*, Brussels: EC.

Expert Working Group on Childcare (1999), *National Childcare Strategy*, Dublin: Stationery Office.

Fahey, T. (1998), "Childcare Policy Options", in *Budget Perspectives*, Proceedings of a Conference held on 27 October 1998, Dublin: ESRI.

Ferber, M.A. (1999), "Introduction", *The Quarterly Review of Economics and Finance*, Vol. 39, pp. 579–595.

Ferber, M.A. and A. Nelson (1999), "Where Do We Go from Here?", *The Quarterly Review of Economics and Finance*, Vol. 39, pp. 781–783.

Fisher, H. (2000), *Investing in People: Family-friendly Work Arrangements in Small and Medium-sized Enterprises*, Dublin: The Equality Authority.

Fynes, B., T. Morrissey, W.K. Roche, B.J. Whelan and J. Williams (1996), *Flexible Working Lives: The Changing Nature of Working Time Arrangements in Ireland*, Dublin: Oak Tree Press.

Ginn, J. et al. (1996), "Feminist Fallacies: A Reply to Hakim on Women's Employment", *British Journal of Sociology*, Vol. 47, No. 1, pp. 167–173.

Goodbody and Associates with T. Fahey and E. Hennessey (1999), *Economics of Childcare*, Dublin: Stationery Office.

Gornick, J.C. and J.A. Jacobs (1996), "A Cross-national Analysis of the Wages of Part-time Workers: Evidence from the United States, the United Kingdom, Canada and Australia", *Work, Employment and Society*, Vol. 10, No. 1, 1–27.

Goss, S. and H. Browne (1991), *Equal Opportunities for Women in the NHS*, London: Department of Health.

Gottschalk, P. and T. Smeeding (1997), "Cross-national Comparisons of Earnings and Income Inequality", *Journal of Economic Literature*, Vol. XXXV, pp. 633–687.

Gunderson, M. (1989), "Male–Female Wage Differentials and Policy Responses", *Journal of Economic Literature*, Vol. 27, No. 1.

Hakim, C. (1992), "Explaining Trends in Occupational Segregation: the Measurement, Causes and Consequences of the Sexual Division of Labour", *European Sociological Review*, Vol. 8, No. 2, pp. 127–152.

Hakim, C. (1993), "Segregated and Integrated Occupations: A New Approach to Analysing Social Change", *European Sociological Review*, Vol. 19, No. 3., p. 289.

Hakim, C. (1996a), *Key Issues in Women's Work: Female Heterogeneity and the Polarisation of Women's Employment*, London: Athlone Press Ltd.

Hakim, C. (1996b), "Labour Mobility and Employment Stability: Rhetoric and Reality on the Sex Differential in Labour Market Behaviour", *European Sociological Review*, Vol. 12, No. 1, pp. 1–31.

Hannan, D., E. Smyth, J. McCullagh, R. O'Leary and D. McMahon (1996), *Co-education and Gender Inequality*, Dublin: Oak Tree Press/ESRI.

Heckman, James J. (1980), "Sample Selection Bias as a Specification Error with an Application to the Estimation of Labor Supply Functions", in James P. Smith (ed.), *Female Labor Supply: Theory and Estimation*, Princeton: Princeton University Press.

ICTU (1987), *Using Job Evaluation to Eliminate Sex Discrimination in Pay*, Dublin: Irish Congress of Trade Unions.

ICTU (1993), *Mainstreaming Equality 1993–98*, Dublin: Irish Congress of Trade Unions.

ICTU (1998), *Delivering Gender Equality, 1999–2004*, Dublin: Irish Congress of Trade Unions.

IPA (1999), *Gender Imbalance in the Irish Civil Service Grades at Higher Executive Officer (HEO) Level and Above*, Executive Summary, Dublin: Institute of Public Administration.

Jenkins, S. (1994), "Earnings Discrimination Measurement: A Distributional Approach," *Journal of Econometrics*, Vol. 61, pp. 105–131.

Jenkins, S. and Symons (1995), "Child Care Costs and Lone Mothers' Employment Rates: UK Evidence", ESRC Working Paper No. 9J-2, Colchester: University of Essex.

Jenson, J. (1989), "The Talents of Women, the Skills of Men: Flexible Specialization and Women", in S. Wood (ed.), *The Transformation of Work?* London: Unwin Hyman.

Juhn, C., K. Murphy and B. Pierce (1991), "Accounting for the Slowdown in Black–White Convergence", in M. Osters (ed.), *Workers and Their Wages*, pp. 107–143, Washington, DC: American Enterprise Institute.

Joshi, H. and P.R. Hinde (1993), "Employment after Childbearing in Post-war Britain: Cohort Study Evidence on Contrasts within and across Generations", *European Sociological Review*, Vol. 9, No. 3, pp. 203–227.

Kidd, M.P. and M. Shannon (1996), "The Gender Wage Gap: A Comparison of Australia and Canada", *Industrial and Labor Relations Review*, Vol. 49, No. 4, pp. 729–746.

Killingsworth, Mark R. (1983), *Labor Supply*, Cambridge: Cambridge University Press.

Layte, R. (1999), *Divided Time: Gender, Paid Employment and Domestic Labour*, Aldershot: Ashgate.

Lazear, E. and S. Rosen (1990), "Male–Female Wage Differentials in Job Ladders", *Journal of Labour Economics* Vol. 8, No. 1, Part 2.

Low Pay Commission (1998), *The National Minimum Wage*, First Report of the Low Pay Commission, Presented to Parliament, June 1998.

McCall, L. (2000), "Gender and the New Inequality; Explaining the College/Non-college Wage Gap", *American Sociological Review*, Vol. 65, pp. 234–255.

McKenna, A. (1990), "Childcare in Ireland 1990", in *Childcare in Ireland: Challenge and Opportunity*, Dublin: Employment Equality Agency.

McRae, S. (1993), "Returning to Work After Childbirth: Opportunities and Inequalities", *European Sociological Review*, Vol. 9, No. 2, 125–138.

McRae, S., H. Joshi and S. Dex (1996), "Employment after Childbearing: A Survival Analysis", *Work, Employment and Society*, Vol. 10, No. 2, pp. 273–296.

Madden, D. (1999), "Towards a Broader Explanation of Male–Female Wage Differences", Centre for Economic Research Working Paper Series 99/11, Department of Economics, University College Dublin.

Makepeace, P. et al. (1999), "How Unequally has Equal Pay Progressed Since the 1970s?" *Journal of Human Resources*, Vol. 34, No. 3, pp. 534–556.

Marini, M.M. (1989), "Sex Differences in Earnings in the United States", *Annual Review of Sociology*, Vol. 15, pp. 343–380.

Marini, M.M. and Brinton M.C. (1984), "Sex Typing in Occupational Socialization", in B.F. Reskin (ed.), *Sex Segregation in the Workplace: Trends, Explanations, Remedies*, Washington, DC: National Academy Press.

Miller, P.W. (1987), "The Effect of the Occupational Segregation of Women in Britain", *Economic Journal*, Vol. 97, No. 388.

Monitoring Committee (1999), *Third Progress Report on the Implementation of the Recommendations of the Second Commission on the Status of Women*, Dublin: Government Publications.

Mroz, Thomas A., (1987), "The Sensitivity of an Empirical Model of Married Women's Hours of Work to Economic and Statistical Assumptions", *Econometrica*, Vol. 55, pp. 765–799.

Murphy, A. and B. Walsh (1996), "The Incidence of Male Non-employment in Ireland", *Economic and Social Review*, Vol. 25, pp. 467–490.

Nakamura, Alice and Masao Nakamura (1983), "Part-time and Full-time Work Behavior of Married Women: A Model with a Doubly Truncated Dependent Variable", *Canadian Journal of Economics*, Vol. 16, pp. 229–157.

NESC (1999), *Opportunities, Challenges and Capacities for Choice*, Dublin: NESC Report No. 149.

Neumark, D. (1988), "Employers' Discriminatory Behavior and the Estimation of Wage Discrimination", *Journal of Human Resources*, Vol. 23, No. 2, pp. 279–295.

Neumark, D. and W. Wascher (1998), "The New Jersey Minimum Wage Experiment: A Re-evaluation Using Payroll Records", Michigan State University, mimeo.

Nolan, B. and G. Hughes (1998), "Competitive Segmented Labour Markets and Exclusion from Retirement Income", ESRI Seminar Paper.

Nolan, B. and B. McCormick (1999), "The Numbers Affected by the Minimum Wage", *Final Report of the Inter-Departmental Group on the Implementation of a National Minimum Wage*, Dublin: Stationery Office.

Oaxaca, R. (1973), "Male–Female Wage Differentials in Urban Labor Markets", *International Economic Review*, Vol. 14, No. 3, pp. 139–148.

O'Brien, J.F. (1981), *A Study of National Wage Agreements in Ireland*, General Research Series Report No. 104, Dublin: The Economic and Social Research Institute.

O'Connell, P.J. (1999), *Adults in Training: An International Comparison*, Paris: OECD.

O'Connell, P.J. and F. McGinnity (1997), *Working Schemes? Active Labour Market Policy in Ireland*, Aldershot: Ashgate.

O'Connell, P.J. and V. Gash (1999), "How Much Does it Cost to Get In? Labour Market Mobility, Working-time and Gender in Ireland", Seminar Paper, Dublin: ESRI.

O'Connor, P. (1995), *The Barriers to Women's Promotion in the Midland and Mid-Western Health Board*, Limerick: Mid-Western Health Board.

O'Connor, P (1996), "Organisational Culture as a Barrier to Women's Promotion", *Economic and Social Review*, Vol. 27, No. 3, pp. 187–216.

O'Connor, P. (1998), *Emerging Voices: Women in Contemporary Irish Society*, Dublin: Institute of Public Administration.

O'Reilly, J. and C. Fagan (1998), *Part-time Prospects: An International Comparison of Part-time Work in Europe, North America and the Pacific Rim*, London: Routledge.

Pencavel, J. (1986), "Labour Supply of Men: A Survey", in O.C. Ashenfelter and R. Layard (eds.), *Handbook of Labour Economics, Vol. 1*, Elsevier.

Petersen, T. and L.A. Morgan (1995), "Separate and Unequal: Occupation–Establishment Sex Segregation and the Gender Wage Gap", *American Journal of Sociology*, Vol. 101, No. 2, pp. 329–365.

Phillips, A. and B. Taylor (1980), "Sex and Skill: Notes Towards a Feminist Economics", *Feminist Review*, No. 6.

Polachek, S.W. (1981), "Occupational Self-selection: A Human Capital Approach to Sex Differences in Occupational Structure", *Review of Economic Statistics*, Vol. 63, pp. 60–69.

Preston, A. (1999), "Occupational Gender Segregation Trends and Explanations", *The Quarterly Review of Economics and Finance*, Vol. 39, pp. 611–624.

Purcell, K., T. Hogarth and C. Simm (1999), *Whose Flexibility? The Costs and Benefits of "Non-Standard" Working Arrangements and Contractual Relations*, Working and Opportunity Series, Joseph Rowntree Foundation.

Reilly, B. (1991), "Occupational Segregation and Selectivity Bias in Occupational Wage Equations: An Empirical Analysis Using Irish Data", *Applied Economics*, Vol. 23.

Roche, W.K. (1994), "The Trend of Unionisation" in T. Murphy and W.K. Roche (eds.), *Irish Industrial Relations in Practice*, Dublin: Oak Tree Press.

Rose, D.L. (1994), "Twenty-five Years Later: Where Do We Stand on Equal Opportunity Law Enforcement?," in P. Burstein (ed.), *Equal Employment Opportunity: Labor Market Discrimination and Public Policy*, Aldine de Gruyter, New York.

Ruane, F.P. and J.M. Sutherland (1999), *Women in the Labour Force*, Dublin: Employment Equality Agency.

Rubery, J. (1980), "Structured Labour Markets, Worker Organization and Low Pay" in A. Amsden (ed.), *The Economics of Women and Work*, Harmondsworth: Penguin.

Rubery, J., M. Smith and C. Fagan (1999), *Women's Employment in Europe: Trends and Prospects*, London: Routledge.

Sexton, J.J. and P.J. O'Connell (eds.) (1996), *Labour Market Studies: Ireland*, Brussels: European Commission.

Sexton, J.J., D. Frost and G. Hughes (1999), *Aspects of Occupational Change in the Irish Economy Recent Trends and Future Prospects*, Dublin: FÁS/ESRI Study No. 7.

SMI Human Resource Management Working Group (2000), *Gender Imbalance in Irish Civil Service Grades at Higher Executive Officer (HEO) Level and Above*, Executive Summary, Dublin: Institute of Public Administration.

Spitze, G. and K. Loscocco (2000), "Women's Position in the Household", *The Quarterly Review of Economics and Finance*, Vol. 39, pp. 647–661.

Suen, E. (1997), "Decomposing Wage Residuals: Unmeasured Skill or Statistical Artifact", *Journal of Labor Economics*, Vol. 15, No. 3, pp. 555–66.

Walby, S. (1986), *Patriarchy at Work: Patriarchal and Capitalist Relations in Employment*, Cambridge: Polity Press.

Whitehouse, G. (1992), "Legislation and Labour Market Gender Inequality: An Analysis of OECD Countries", *Work, Employment and Society*, Vol. 6, No. 1, pp. 65–86.

Williams, J. and C. Collins (1998), "Childcare Arrangements in Ireland: A Report to the Commission on the Family", in *Strengthening Families for Life*, final report of the Commission on the Family.

Working Group on Childcare Facilities for Working Parents (1994), *Report to the Minister for Equality and Law Reform*, Dublin: Stationery Office.

Wright, R.E. and J.F. Ermisch (1991), "Gender Discrimination in the British Labour Market: A Reassessment", *Economic Journal*, Vol. 101, May, pp. 508–522.

Zabalza, A. and Z. Tzannatos (1985), *Women and Equal Pay: The Effects of Legislation on Female Employment and Wages in Britain*, Cambridge: Cambridge University Press.